— PERIOD —
FIREPLACES

—Period—
Fireplaces

A PRACTICAL GUIDE TO
PERIOD-STYLE DECORATING

Judith Miller

MITCHELL BEAZLEY

First published in Great Britain in 1995 by Mitchell Beazley
an imprint of Reed Consumer Books Limited,
Michelin House,
81 Fulham Road, London SW3 6RB
and Auckland, Melbourne, Singapore and Toronto

Chief Contributor: **John Wainwright**

Editor: **Nina Sharman**
Art Editor: **Lisa Tai**
Production: **Heather O'Connoll**

Executive Editor: **Judith More**
Art Director: **Jacqui Small**
Executive Art Editor: **Larraine Shamwana**

Special photography: **Michael Crockett**
Styling for special photography: **Melanie Molesworth**
Colour Illustrations: **Coral Mula**
Front jacket photograph: **James Merrell**
Back jacket photographs: **Kim Sayer**
Installation of Edwardian Fireplace: **Amazing Grates**

A CIP record for this book is available from the British Library

ISBN 1 85732 397 1

The publishers have made every effort to ensure that all instructions given in this book
are accurate and safe, but they cannot accept liability for any resulting injury, damage or
loss to either person or property whether direct or consequential and howsoever arising.

Produced by Mandarin Offset
Printed and bound in Hong Kong

Contents

Foreword

Following the Second World War there was an understandable and widespread desire to rebuild or modernize much of the housing stock. While many period homes were raised to the ground, most survived but were subjected to significant alteration (at the time of writing there are still some six million buildings in Great Britain alone that were constructed prior to 1920). Apart from necessities such as the renewal of worn out and often inadequate electrical circuits and plumbing systems, most of these alterations were made for a mixture of aesthetic and practical reasons, and largely involved the ripping-out, replacement or boxing-in of original fixtures and fittings.

Notable "improvements", among many, were the removal of fireplaces thought to be rendered obsolete by the installation of central heating, the renewal of often intricate and finely detailed plaster mouldings with smooth skimmed plaster, the boxing in of period joinery (especially stair rails and panelled doors) with sheets of plain hardboard, and the replacement of original bath wares and light fixtures with more modern counterparts. Changing fashions also resulted in the introduction of decorative schemes that, in terms of furniture, textiles, patterns and colours, bore little relation to those in vogue when the houses were originally built.

To condemn such changes and alterations on purist grounds would be to misunderstand the nature of housing. Most houses gradually evolve over time to meet the changing requirements of new owners. For example, rooms are added to provide extra accommodation, or converted for a different use – such as bedrooms into bathrooms, or separate kitchens and dining rooms knocked through into one large eat-in kitchen.

This process of continual renewal and up-dating was as familiar to the Elizabethans, the Georgians and the Victorians as it is to us in the 20th century. Moreover, many of the changes and alterations made have not been new or innovative. Fashion and design have always drawn heavily on the past for inspiration: the Victorians, in particular, borrowed and adapted numerous ideas from previous centuries, notably when it came to the production of furniture, textiles and architectural details. Ultimately whether one likes or dislikes particular changes is a matter of personal aesthetics. However, since the middle of the 1970s there has been a fairly broad consensus that a large number of structural and decorative alterations made between 1945 and the 1960s have been undesirable. The main complaint is that too many of them have been unsympathetic to the structure, style and character of the house.

As a consequence, home owners and property developers have set about restoring many original features and redecorating in styles that are more appropriate to the period of the house in question. This has been an almost universally popular development – certainly if judged only by the fact that "authentically restored" houses command (often substantially) higher prices than those that have been, in estate agent's/realtor's parlance, "completely modernized".

As more and more home owners come to realize that such restorations not only improve their immediate surroundings, but are also a satisfying and rewarding activity, there has been a commensurate growth in the number of companies selling original and reproduction fixtures and fittings and decorating materials. Restoration is thus not only seen as desirable, but is also increasingly easy to achieve. I hope that this book will make it even easier.

In the first half of the book, the numerous illustrations and accompanying text tracing the development of the fireplace through the centuries will help you to choose the right fireplace for the various rooms throughout your house. In the second half, the practical information and illustrated step-by-step projects guide you through the processes of installation, restoration and decoration.

I hope that this book will prove to be not only an invaluable guide to restoring period houses, but also provide you with the inspiration and guidance to tackle many projects that hitherto you might have felt were beyond your abilities – if my own experience over the last 20 years is anything to go by, I think you will be pleasantly surprised at what you can achieve.

JUDITH MILLER

Introduction

In *A Letter to Lord Byron* (1937), the English poet W. H. Auden wrote:

"Preserve me above all from central heating.
It may be D.H. Lawrence hocus-pocus
But I prefer a room that's got a focus."

In the decades that followed the Second World War, but particularly during the 1960s, it seemed that Auden was in something of a minority. The ever-increasing efficiency and affordability of coal, gas and oil central heating systems, and individual gas and electric fires, resulted in the boarding or bricking up of original fireplaces in numerous houses. At the same time, fire-surrounds (mantelpieces) were sometimes left in place purely as decorative features, removed altogether, or replaced with a "modern" alternative that, in terms of design, often bore little or no relation either to the original it had replaced or the architectural style of the house in question. (For a typical example, see the York stone fireplace installed during the early 1970s in the dining room of a suburban Edwardian house on page 86.)

At the time, and even with hindsight, the practical incentives for making such changes were both obvious and understandable. Modern gas and electric fires and central heating were simply more user-friendly than traditional coal- and log-burning fires. All the former required of the home owner was the pressing of a switch to

Right: *A typical example of a grand, 16th-century English fireplace. The hearth and the cheeks of the opening are of local stone and brick (respectively). Similarly, the wooden lintel will have almost certainly been cut from home-grown timber. However, the ornate extended chimneypiece, like many others installed in large houses during the 16th and 17th centuries, was the product of European craftsmen and imported from either Italy, Spain, Portugal or France.*

Left: *A simple kitchen fireplace c.1790. As was often the case with smaller fireplaces in lesser dwellings, the wooden mantel shelf has quite plain mouldings, and is nailed to the chimney breast rather than being supported on a pair of jambs. The iron andirons and swivel crane are from the same period – the latter designed to support pots and kettles for open-hearth cooking.*

Left: *Although partly restored, this open-hearth fireplace in the basement of a mid-18th-century house retains most of its original features. Aside from the cooking accessories within the hearth, numerous other items of kitchenalia are hung from hooks on the wooden mantel shelf – a practical and decorative means of storage in a busy working kitchen.*

produce a virtually instantaneous and regular output of heat. Coal and log fires, on the other hand, were much more labour-intensive. In addition to maintaining a "coal house" or damp-free space inside or underneath the house for the storage of fuel, the householder had to carry heavy coals and logs (after the latter had been chopped up to a suitable size) to the various hearths throughout the property. Having done that, the fires had to be prepared for lighting each day with paper balls or kindling, or both, and the ashes and cinders from the previous day's fire swept up and taken away. Once lit,

coal and log fires also needed regular attention – more fuel having to be added at the right time in order to maintain an even output of heat.

Apart from the preparation and maintenance involved in burning traditional fires, there was also the problem of pollution to contend with. In urban areas during much of the 19th and 20th centuries, coal-burning fires had made a substantial contribution to the build-up of atmospheric pollution which, during adverse weather conditions, sometimes resulted in dense smogs enveloping cities and large towns, often for weeks at a time. The elderly, and people

Above: *Dating from c.1738, this American Colonial fireplace survives in the small drawing room of Drayton Hall, near Charleston, South Carolina. The elaborately carved, painted wooden overmantel reflects the classical European influence prevalent throughout the southern Colonies.*

Left: *Painted wall panelling and architrave, incorporating simple mouldings, are typical of Colonial houses on the Eastern seaboard.*

with respiratory problems, proved particularly vulnerable – to the extent that the rates of sickness and even death among such groups rose dramatically during these periods.

While the introduction of various pollution controls and Clean Air Acts, together with the development of smokeless fuels during the 1950s, mitigated much of this problem, they did not alter the fact that the smoke and dust generated by burning coal (and to a lesser extent wood) in open fires had an accumulative and adverse effect on decorations and soft furnishings inside the home. Quite simply, in winter they became dirtier far quicker, and required cleaning or renewing more often, than during the summer months when the fires remained unlit.

It is easy to underestimate just how ingrained with dirt and dust wallpapers and fabrics could become under these circumstances. For example, when many people conjure up a typical Victorian or Edwardian interior they usually imagine a rather dark, gloomy room dominated by dull and dingy colours in a range of tones that are perhaps best associated with a bowl of brown

Windsor soup. However, many Victorian and Edwardian rooms were decorated in a wide range of bright colours and patterns. They did not, unfortunately, stay that way for very long, and many of the interiors that survived had lost much of their original vibrancy of colour under accumulative layers of smoke and coal dust by the time they were recorded for posterity in early colour photographs.

Aside from such practical considerations, the boxing-in or complete removal of original fireplaces during the twenty to thirty years after 1945 also took place for aesthetic reasons. Elaborately embellished fire-surrounds that projected out from chimney breasts and into the living space of a room, especially when accompanied by all the paraphernalia (fenders, brushes, tongs, shovels, scuttles, etc.) associated with the traditional hearth, did not fit happily into the clean lines and relatively unadorned surfaces that were such a feature of the decorative schemes favoured by architects and designers working under the umbrella of the Modernist movement. In other words, traditional fireplaces fell out of fashion in favour of slim, wall-mounted panel radiators and relatively discreet chrome, beaten copper and stove-enamelled gas and electric fires (free-standing or wall-mounted).

Since around the mid-1970s, however, such "improvements" or modernizations have come to be considered something of a mistake, and Auden's preference for a room with a focus has gained a ground swell of support from people who live in period houses and from people who want to create a period style in their home. There are a number of reasons for this development. First, the removal or boarding-up of a fireplace significantly detracts from the intended architectural proportions of a room – with the original focal point gone it does not feel right; there is something missing. Second, however efficient a central heating system is, it does not seem to compensate for the inability of home owners to gather round an identifiable source of heat. Gathering round a fire when it is cold and dark outside is a very primitive instinct that appears to have survived the advances of modern technology – almost certainly because it promotes a feeling of coziness and a sense of well-being and security. Third, the modern gas and electric fires that work without producing a traditional flame somehow fail to kindle the primitive emotions that are stirred by a blazing coal or log fire.

These realizations have, over the last fifteen years or so, resulted in a widespread opening up and installation of original and reproduction fireplaces. Architectural salvage companies have made good profits from selling and installing original fireplaces that were torn out during the drive to modernize. Where the demand for original fireplaces has exceeded supply, other manufacturers have produced a wide range of high-quality, authentic-looking, reproduction fireplaces in marble, cast-iron and wood at competitive prices. This development has been undoubtedly further fuelled over recent years by the considerable improvements designers and manufacturers have made to "real flame" coal and log gas fires. Numerous models have been produced in a wide range of period styles that can be successfully combined with period fire-surrounds. As a result, the home owner can have his or her cake and eat it: no lugging around heavy coals and logs, no smoke and dust to spoil the upholstery, but "real" coals and logs, efficient heat and real flames.

This book has been designed to help the householder who wants to install or restore a period fireplace in their home. Thus, the first four chapters trace all aspects (structural and

Left: *An authentic and high-quality, 20th-century reproduction of an early 17th-century carved oak chimneypiece.*

Above: *A 20th-century reproduction of a late 18th-century, Adam-inspired, fireplace, combining wood and marble.*

decorative) of the development of the fireplace – century by century – from medieval times to the present day. Both the text and the accompanying illustrations are primarily intended to be used as reference material to help you to match the right style of fireplace to the various rooms in your home.

The second half of the book has a more practical bent. In addition to showing you how traditional coal and log open fires work, and what must be done to ensure that they function both efficiently and safely, there is also an illustrated step-by-step project on installing an Edwardian fireplace and equipping it with a gas-fired coal-effect burner unit. (The instructions can be adapted for the installation of various other period fireplaces, particularly those designed during the 19th century, and cover the numerous aspects of the process that you can safely tackle yourself, and also those that should or must be left to a qualified professional.)

As well as installing a fireplace, there are illustrated instructions on the care, repair and restoration of a range of materials including marble, cast-iron, slate stone and wooden fire-surrounds, plus step-by-step projects on faux marbling (simulating marble using paints and glazes), stripping, staining and antiquing wooden surrounds, repairing ceramic tiles, and making a decorative Victorian fire screen (using modern MDF – medium density fibreboard – and the traditional technique of découpage). Also included is an illustrated section on how to go about dressing a fireplace with both decorative and practical objects, and in a style that is appropriate to different historical periods.

Finally, at the back of the book there is a comprehensive directory of the names and addresses of leading manufacturers, specialist suppliers and installers of both original and reproduction period fireplaces and their various component parts.

Left: *A substantial early 17th-century stone fireplace in the main drawing room of Plas Teg, North Wales. The jambs, four-centred arch, lintel and mantel shelf were carved as separate sections and assembled with mortar on site.*

Right: *An early Victorian marble fireplace. In the lesser rooms of many 19th-century houses, chimney-pieces were often made of wood and faux marbled with paint in a simulation of the natural (and more expensive) stone.*

Anatomy of a fireplace

Technological developments and changing fashions in architecture and design have resulted in the production of numerous fireplace styles, however their basic structure has altered very little since the 15th century.

Fuel is placed within a non-combustible enclosure, which is open to the room and the flue and chimney above, and generally set flush against a wall or within a projecting chimney breast. The hearth is made of stone, brick, slate or ceramic tiles. The splayed sides, or cheeks, are made of brick, stone, fireproof cement, or tiles. The back can be exposed or rendered brickwork (protected by an iron fireback), or fireproof cement in a cast-iron framework.

Logs were traditionally placed directly on the hearth, and held in position with a pair of iron fire dogs (andirons). Initially, coal was burnt in an iron basket called a dog grate, but these were gradually superseded by the cast-iron register grate (incorporating an adjustable vent designed to regulate the flow of air). A metal fender prevented burning coals from rolling off the hearth.

A chimneypiece consists of a pair of jambs (the sides) which support a horizontal lintel or frieze. Jambs can take the form of columns, pilasters, carved figures or simple architectural mouldings, depending on the style. The degree of ornamentation on the frieze or lintel also reflects the rest of the fire-surround. The areas between the jambs and the fireplace opening (the slips) are often faced with decorative marble, slate or ceramic tiles. Where the fireplace opening is arched, the triangular areas above the arch and below the frieze or lintel are known as spandrels. Usually augmented with brackets secured to the tops of the jambs, the lintel or frieze can provide support for a mantel shelf which, in turn, may support a decorative overmantel – the latter often incorporating a mirror, a frame for a picture, or shelving.

Chimneypieces are traditionally made of marble, stone, slate, cast iron or wood. With the exception of cast-iron, which are largely of one-piece construction, all the components of a chimneypiece are made separately and glued, bolted, screwed or nailed together on site.

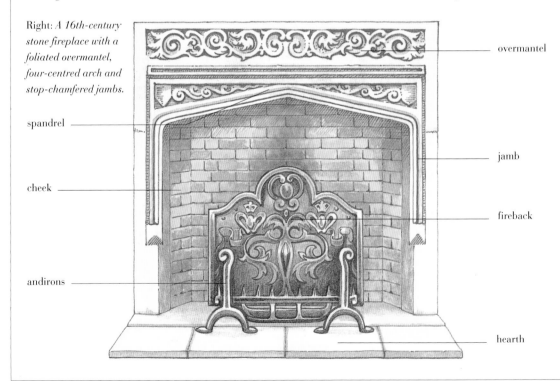

Right: *A 16th-century stone fireplace with a foliated overmantel, four-centred arch and stop-chamfered jambs.*

overmantel

spandrel

cheek

andirons

jamb

fireback

hearth

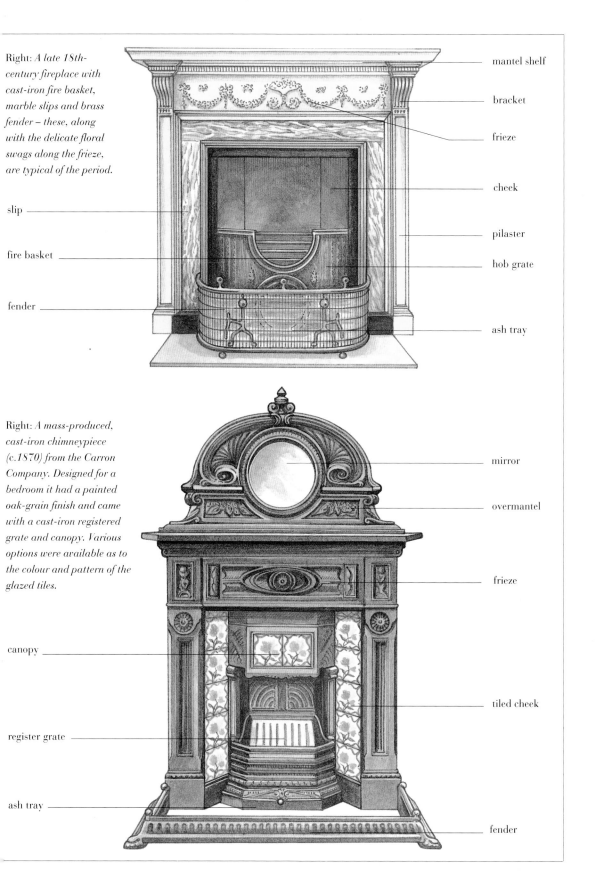

Right: *A late 18th-century fireplace with cast-iron fire basket, marble slips and brass fender – these, along with the delicate floral swags along the frieze, are typical of the period.*

mantel shelf

bracket

frieze

slip

cheek

fire basket

pilaster

hob grate

fender

ash tray

Right: *A mass-produced, cast-iron chimneypiece (c.1870) from the Carron Company. Designed for a bedroom it had a painted oak-grain finish and came with a cast-iron registered grate and canopy. Various options were available as to the colour and pattern of the glazed tiles.*

mirror

overmantel

canopy

frieze

register grate

tiled cheek

ash tray

fender

FIREPLACE
STYLES

Early Fireplaces

Up until the late 15th century a central open hearth remained the most common form of fireplace. In the medieval manor houses of England the open fire was situated toward the upper end of the communal living hall, the smoke drifted up through a hole in the roof. However, the increasing use of hoods or canopies, initially made from wattle-and-daub, and designed to channel smoke more efficiently away from the room, resulted in a gradual relocation of the fireplace to a wall – it was easier to support a hood there, rather than from a wooden panel or the ceiling.

Consequently, by the beginning of the 16th century the open hearth had been superseded in most houses by the enclosed wall fireplace – a process given additional impetus, following the Reformation, by the abolition of a tax imposed from Rome on the building of chimneys.

THE 16TH CENTURY

The simplest wall fireplaces consisted of brick or stone stacks (chimneys), either built against an outside wall or on one of the central, internal walls. Back-to-back fireplaces, or those situated directly above or below each other, shared the same flue which would conduct the smoke to a louvre in the roof. The hearth was recessed in an opening at the bottom of the stack, and made of brick or stone – the back wall often finished with either thin bricks or tiles laid on edge, or protected by an iron fireback. The simplest hearths housed small brick walls to support the logs, but most had a pair of iron firedogs (andirons) for this purpose. Early firedogs were joined together at the base by a bar which went across the front of the fire. However, by the end of the 16th century the two firedogs stood separately.

Above: A typical 16th-century inglenook fireplace. The brick canopy positioned directly above the middle of the hearth was a reasonably common feature of inglenooks during this period. Colloquially known as a "beehive" because of its cylindrical shape, it was designed to maximize the up-draught and minimize the amount of smoke that might drift back into the room.

Above: A restored 16th-century inglenook. The lintel and other exposed beams would originally have been untreated – staining or painting them black was a Victorian fashion.

Left: A 17th-century brick and stone fireplace. The hearth opening is, typically, surmounted by a substantial hand-carved lintel and mantel shelf.

In lesser houses, the opening for the hearth at the base of the chimney was spanned by a simple stone or wooden lintel, which could be either plain, chamfered, moulded or carved. However, in grander houses the hearth was usually spanned by a more elaborate four-centred arch with chamfered or moulded decoration. There were other embellishments, which reflected the status and wealth of the Tudor householder, including brightly gilded and painted heraldic badges, shields, or mottoes on the lintels, and maker's names, dates of manufacture, and family crests and initials on the iron firebacks. Andirons also became increasingly elaborate. However, it was the development and adornment of the fire surround, and the area above it that elevated the fireplace to the dominant architectural feature within the house.

The Tudor fireplace had, in some respects, been treated as no more than part of a panelled wall, subsequently, the growth and development of Renaissance ideas about architecture and design throughout Europe resulted in the fireplace becoming a substantial feature in its own right. More specifically, the Italians devised a basic form for the fireplace – one that has remained fashionable ever since – which comprised a projecting chimney-breast with an elaborate surround. The area above the opening, on the front of the chimney-breast, being the site for ornament, which could either be architectural or sculptural in character, or both.

In England, the first results, installed by itinerant Italian or local craftsmen, appeared in the great Elizabethan manor houses, where the fireplace, flanked by columns, half-columns or pilasters, and an entablature with highly ornamented carved wooden panels above, became the focal point of rooms that were already elaborately decorated. This type of surround, often massive and with a large opening of tall proportions, was also installed in larger Jacobean houses, with the owner's coat-of-arms often carved in the panel above the fire.

Above: *An early 16th-century fireplace with the unusual combination of rubbed-brick jambs surmounted by a carved wooden lintel. The cast-iron hood, and the small firebasket for burning coals, are later additions.*

Right: *A monumental Jacobean stone fireplace (c.1602–10), the focal point of the Great Chamber at Chastleton House in Oxfordshire. The overmantel incorporates a carved central panel bearing the coat-of-arms of the original owner of the house.*

THE 17TH CENTURY

Throughout the 17th century, a period largely dominated, architecturally, by the classically-inspired and flamboyant ornamentation of Baroque, it remained usual to give the fireplace a prestigious treatment in houses of any pretension. White marble, or contrasting coloured marbles, were thus increasingly favoured over wood or brick. However, there was a move, primarily led by French architects such as Jean Babet, Pierre Colot and Jean Cotelle, to make the massive, Italian-inspired chimneypieces which were being produced in Europe around 1620 more compact, and the ornamentation better integrated with the structure.

The results included the addition of a frieze or cornice, or an overmantel, the latter usually framed by pilasters and sometimes pedimented. During the first half of the 17th century the best and most elaborate cornices projected on corbels forward of the pilasters, thereby transforming the overmantel into a sculptural feature. Naturalistic carving, for example in the manner of Grinling Gibbons, was also used extensively, the overmantel being richly sculpted with mythological figures, fruit, foliage and dead game birds. (In England, after the Restoration, carved frames became enlarged, while the panels they framed were reduced in size.)

There was also a fashion, in the latter part of the 17th century, for using (very expensive) mirror glass in overmantels – a sign of real wealth. Pictures, painted specifically, were also set into the chimney breast. In England, architects such as Inigo Jones, John Webb, Sir Christopher Wren and Sir Roger Pratt adopted such devices in creating a marginally more restrained English Baroque style of chimneypiece, many of which were diagonally placed across the corners of rooms when space was at a premium.

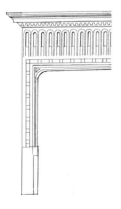

Above: *A stylish but not entirely harmonious mid-17th-century, provincial, marble chimneypiece.*

Right: *A mid-17th-century fireplace with a sumptuously carved marble achievement of arms on the overmantel.*

Left to right: *The Classical influence indicated by frieze and cornice on an early 17th-century surround; elaborately carved stone pilasters, frieze and cornice (c.1664); a delicately carved corner surround (c.1670); and a plain marble panel stopped by scrolls and surmounted by a cornice (c.1685).*

In the Netherlands the chimney-breast was cut back at the fire-opening, in effect, to form a hood, which was supported on columns or brackets. Less flamboyant than many of their European counterparts, these more restrained Dutch fireplaces incorporated a heavy cornice or mantel shelf, but little or no ornament above it. They often featured a linen pelmet – a *tours de cheminees* – attached to the underside of the overhang, to help trap the rising smoke. (It was detachable, and therefore washable.) This was the forerunner to the Victorian mantel frill. On the other side of the hearth, within the hooded space, it was common to line the wall with delft-ware tiles, either plain white or with blue figures – an idea brought back to England by Sir William Brereton.

In the American Colonies during the 17th century, the fireplace always received some decorative emphasis. However, the promotion of the hearth to the most important internal feature of a house – as it had become in Europe – did not occur until the 18th century, when the kitchen and other living rooms were separated, leaving the parlour fireplace unconstrained by the demands of cooking. However, while English styles were popular in the southern colonies, where most of the gentry class were English, up until the Revolutionary period the earliest substantial houses only had a large open brick hearth in the main living area, sometimes with a bake oven at the back. Such fireplaces tended to be dirty and inefficient, and decoration was limited to a moulded lintel or rough surround and patterns laid in the brick-work. In America it was only right at the end of the 17th century that fire-surrounds with heavy bolection mouldings became common, and the fireplace assumed the focal point in halls, parlours, dining rooms and other important rooms of the grandest houses.

Above: *Chimney hoods survived well into the 17th century, and were often combined with pilasters, frieze and cornice to form imposing, tomb-like compositions.*

Above: *An elaborate, Italian, 17th-century Baroque chimneypiece. Sculpted from Verona marble, it was eventually exported to England.*

Left: *A bizarre use of ornament indicates the work of a provincial designer with a shaky grasp of antique detail.*

Right: *A large, North American hall fireplace (c.1698) with heavy bolection mouldings and marbled paintwork.*

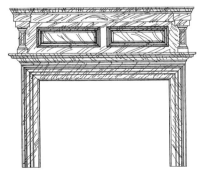

Left: *A substantial, late 17th-century fireplace that, like many others of the period, has contrasting coloured and patterned marbles. The arched pediment breaking forward of the cornice lends additional weight and presence to the overall composition of the surround.*

Below: *Simple but elegant stone panelling, combined with architrave embellished with multiple mouldings, lends an understated Classical elegance to what is an otherwise a rather ordinary hearth and opening.*

Above: *A sketch of a Baroque fireplace by Christopher Wren. The details of carving were drawn by Grinling Gibbons.*

Right: *Although of simple design, this mid-17th-century fireplace is dignified by the juxtaposition of different marbles.*

THE IMPEDIMENTA OF THE HEARTH

Throughout Europe, cast-iron fire-backs became almost universal in larger houses. Typically arched in form, they were decorated in relief with either the family's coat-of-arms, or favourite ornamental themes taken from the Bible or Classical mythology. Rich floral borders were also characteristic of the period. Where wood was burned, the fire-backs had to be large and wide, but for coal, which was becoming cheaper and more practical in cities and towns, they could be narrow and taller in proportion.

Again, where wood was the fuel, firedogs remained a necessary means of propping up the logs and keeping them in place, as in the 16th century. Ordinary versions were still made of iron. However, better quality ones had brass or silver mounts, which reflected the firelight pleasingly. Toward the latter half of the 17th century firedogs gradually decreased in size, because of the lower openings of fireplaces, and simpler forms, such as balusters, finial-like shapes and globes, became fashionable. Where sea coal was the fuel, dog grates, or fire baskets, made of wrought iron were employed to keep the hot coals from falling forward onto the floor. Some incorporated receptacles for warming bottles and jugs of wine. Additional devices included bellows, billets, tongs, shovels and brushes.

Fireplaces with large openings tended to be draughty during the summer months, when the fire was not lit. Consequently, a chimney board was used to cover the gap. These could be made of timber or sheet metal, but more usually at this time canvas stretched over a wooden frame, and they were invariably lavishly decorated.

Another feature developed for the fireplace during the 17th century, was the clay bread oven, an early ancestor of the kitchen range. This was a British invention, found especially in Devon and Cornwall, but exported to North America not that long after the Pilgrim fathers landed. The oven was often accompanied by a built-in box for keeping salt dry and a fireside spice cupboard.

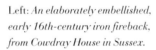

Left: An elaborately embellished, early 16th-century iron fireback, from Cowdray House in Sussex.

Right: As with the example shown left, a crest, the initials of the owner and the date of manufacture are typical of better firebacks.

Right: A 17th-century, arch-topped, cast-iron fireback, decorated with an allegorical figure of Spring. The richly ornamented borders, displaying floral, shell and maritime motifs, are a common embellishment of this period.

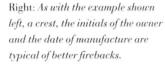

Below: Two 17th-century andirons, or firedogs. Used in pairs, they were designed to prevent logs rolling off the hearth. Most were made of cast or wrought iron, although the better examples often featured brass or even silver mounts.

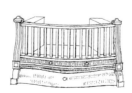

Above: A French fireplace, c.1661, with a lavishly decorated chimney board.

Above: A late 17th-century basket grate designed for burning sea coal.

18th-Century Fireplaces

The richness and complexity of many late-17th-century fireplace designs still found favour during the early 18th century. Such designs are perhaps best exemplified by those incorporated in Daniel Marot's grandly conceived, continental Baroque schemes for French and English salons. Up until the 1730s chimneypieces displaying Baroque details, such as richly carved lintels showing symmetrical stems and scrolling acanthus leaves emerging from a central basket, were still being produced. Although the chimneypiece remained the focal point of the main living room in grand houses during the early 18th century, it was no longer quite such an obtrusive feature as it had been in the 17th century.

There were a number of reasons for this development. Firstly, a large, centrally placed chimney

An early Georgian, canted (corner) fireplace with a *shallow cupboard built into the chimney breast.*

stack – found in most of the bigger Tudor and Jacobean houses – looked somewhat ungainly in the new and often smaller classically-inspired houses being constructed in the 18th century. One of the solutions architects employed to overcome this was to site some fireplaces at each of the four corners of the house or at the gable ends (a process that had begun in the 17th century).

Secondly, in England coal became an increasingly popular and less expensive alternative to wood, particularly by the second half of the 18th century. Consequently, the fireplace itself was gradually set further back which meant a narrower flue that provided the draw necessary for the burning of coal. This meant that in thinner-walled brick buildings the chimney stack formed a projection on the outside rather than the inside wall.

Thirdly, in France, and in countries where French designs were taken up, fireplaces were proportionately lower and their openings smaller – the latter again necessary for burning coal rather than wood. The highly decorative and ornamental compositions above them were also disappearing and gradually being replaced by a large area of mirror-glass which, in terms of its shape and the frame around it, formed part of the mural decoration of the room as a whole. In French pattern books of the time, separate designs for chimneypieces now rarely appeared, as they had done in the 17th century. Instead, the fireplace was depicted as an integral part of the whole wall.

However, while the fireplace gradually became less physically obtrusive during the 18th century, it nevertheless remained, wherever it was sited, the visual centrepiece of the early Georgian room. In England and Germany, the old tradition of publishing separate designs for chimneypieces continued, and the incorporation of striking ornamental features on the chimney breast remained popular in grander houses for longer than it did in France. Also, in the streets of fashionable, middle- and upper-middle class houses that were appearing in ever-greater numbers, fireplaces became increasingly sophisticated, reflecting the designs of those found in grand houses.

Above: *An aesthetically pure (austere), marble surround from the 1720s. The "swan's nest" grate is c.1770, or later.*

Left: *Also 1720-30, this marble fire-surround displays typically robust decorative details.*

The brick arch and jambs are revealed beneath the wooden mantel shelf of this 1720s fireplace.

An elegant wooden sur-round, c.1725, with flat jambs and lintel – the latter with a serpentine profile.

EARLY GEORGIAN

In England during the first half of the 18th century, the fireplace designs of Inigo Jones (1578–1652) – which were still widely circulated in pattern books – proved very influential, and Classical features were much in evidence The finest chimneypieces were made of carved white statuary marble, and often featured inlays of coloured marbles or rare materials such as porphyry. Typical fireplace surrounds took the form of a heavy but very narrow shelf supported on architectural jambs, scrolled brackets or consoles or, in the very finest examples, carved caryatid figures. (Leading architect and designer William Kent often used flanking herms – busts on pillars, and a favourite Palladian form – for this purpose.) Alternative popular designs for surrounds during the first half of the century were less voluptuously sculptural and more finely detailed: mouldings such as egg-and-dart, for example, were used to enclose finely figured and often colourful marble cheeks or slips (the strips that were used to fill the space between the surround and the grate). Plain or decorative tiled slips were also much in evidence, as they had been in the latter part of the 17th century.

A 1739 stepped and eared lintel by William Jones.

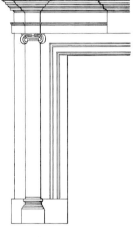

An enervated Ionic column, c.1751.

Console jambs and carved lintel, c.1744, William Kent.

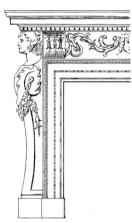

Flanking herms were a favourite Palladian form.

Left: A splendid and rare example of a George II (1727-1760), Siena marble chimneypiece, originally installed in a substantial house in Wiltshire. The Classical lines and proportions of the surround are echoed in the carved plaque in the middle of the frieze, which depicts that popular fable from ancient Rome: Androcles and the Lion.

In the less important rooms of grander houses, or in middle-class homes, scagliola (imitation marble) was sometimes used as an inexpensive alternative to marble. Similarly, most of the popular marble fireplace designs were also made in wood in sections and featured carved or applied composition details. The wood was invariably of ordinary quality but, like doors and wall-panelling, painted to resemble the more fashionable and expensive materials of the time: namely, various marbles and finely figured hardwoods. Simple country fireplaces, on the other hand, often had just a stout wooden lintel above the opening, as they had done during the previous two centuries.

On the chimney breast above the surround, in the grander English houses, there was usually a bold architectural composition which sometimes incorporated mirror-glass. More common, however, was a painting or picture panel designed to echo the door case of the room (especially in neo-Palladian designs) or a sculptured relief. In the case of the latter, scenes from Classical mythology were prevalent, as they were on the surround. Other popular motifs included masks and swags, also favoured by the Palladians, while complete

Left: *The softwood chimneypiece and surrounding wall panelling of this early to mid-Georgian sitting room have been wood-grained to simulate mahogany.*

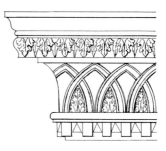

Above: *Two "Gothic cornices" from Batty Langley's* Builder's Director or Bench-Mate *of 1751.*

Above left: *Detail of richly carved lintel, c.1730s, in the Baroque style.*

Left: *A Classical mask and swags from a finely carved Palladian lintel, and a lion mask – the latter often used as a central motif on 1730s chimneypieces.*

designs for Rococo fantasies in Gothic and Chinese styles were produced around the middle of the 18th century, in the manner of Thomas Chippendale, by the likes of W. Ince. (Some Gothic chimneypiece designs were based on medieval tombs: one of the best examples being in the Great Parlour at Strawberry Hill, in Twickenham, England, which was designed by Richard Bentley in the early 1750s.)

The depiction of mythological scenes on classically-inspired fireplaces was not without controversy. In England, for example, Isaac Ware, the architect, felt that it was necessary to warn people of the embarrassment that "nudities" could cause. He wrote: "In a chimneypiece they would be abominable" and he insisted that "some drapery is always to be allowed. The question is how much and in what manner". He asserted: "shewing a thigh is contrary to ... modesty", whereas if "drapery be executed well, and the limbs will be seen through it: there will be at once elegance and decency".

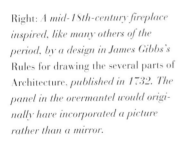

Above: Designed by Richard Bentley in 1753-4, this splendid wooden Gothic chimneypiece was inspired by a medieval tomb and installed in the Great Parlour of Horace Walpole's house, Strawberry Hill, in Twickenham just outside London.

Right: A mid-18th-century fireplace inspired, like many others of the period, by a design in James Gibbs's Rules for drawing the several parts of Architecture, published in 1732. The panel in the overmantel would originally have incorporated a picture rather than a mirror.

Above left: *A plain but functional fireplace in a housekeeper's room – sited in the semi-basement of a late Georgian townhouse.*

Left: *A late 18th-century fireplace with Classical detailing typical of the period. The slips and hearth are in contrasting coloured and patterned marbles.*

Below left: *A reproduction, late 18th-century fireplace, with finely carved Classical*

decoration on the surround and a particularly elegant polished cast-iron, arch-topped hearth opening and fire basket.

Above right: *A popular mid-18th-century design, in the style of William Kent. Shells, rosettes, and swags and tails were typical embellishments for the frieze.*

Below right: *A finely carved cast-iron insert within a plain marble surround.*

LATE GEORGIAN

The main development in fireplace design during the second half of the 18th century was a consolidation of the taste for classically-inspired forms. This was primarily due to the profound influence of Robert and James Adam, the chief exponents of Classical designs, together with a tendency toward suppressing architectural features inside the house. As a result, fashionable chimneypieces were given a simple and strictly rectilinear treatment: namely, pilasters or consoles supporting an entablature with a ledge or shelf above the fire (a model that remained in favour throughout most of the 19th century). Where flues were being built much deeper into the wall, thereby doing away with the need for a chimney breast, fireplaces thus became relatively unobtrusive apertures in the wall.

However, while fashionable fireplaces of the second half of the century became simpler in form, they remained enriched with ornament. The range of classically-inspired fireplaces on the market from the 1760s onward was enormous. The finest examples were made of white marble, often with coloured or black and white inner slips, and appeared in the most important rooms of grand and smaller houses alike. Replicas in stone, sometimes enriched with inlays of different coloured marbles, and wood were also widely available, the latter often painted white, or

Left: A reproduction of an Adam-style fireplace which provides the focal point in this late Georgian interior.

Above: A fine example of an Adam fireplace. The quality of decorative paint-work and carving is superb.

Above: Illustrations showing typical Classical motifs – such as Helios, the sun god, in his chariot – found on the grandest 18th-century chimneypieces.

Right: A late 18th-century marble fireplace, with a French-Empire inspired mirror, and an unusual serpentine-profile steel fender of the period.

marbled as earlier in the century. Regardless of the basic material, all such fireplaces were embellished with a range of Classical motifs, notably medallions, swags, ribbons, urns, lyres, masks, corner paterae, foliage, and cameos of fine ceramics. Josiah Wedgwood produced inlaid marble chimneypieces decorated with Wedgwood plaques, from designs by John Flaxman; their jambs typically in the form of architectural pilasters. Sphinxes or Helios, the sun god, in his chariot were also popular subjects found on the grandest chimneypieces.

While Classical restraint was sometimes abandoned in favour of fancy or exotic styles, such as Rococo, Chinoiserie or Hindu, and while richly painted Pompeian and Etruscan motifs became fashionable in the 1770s, generally speaking surrounds became more austerely Classical toward the end of the century. These were best seen in the strict geometric lines of, for example, Sir John Soane's Greek Revival designs, with their Greek key marble inlays (or painted imitations). But throughout the period, regardless of the degree of flamboyance or austerity of the surround, a mirror-glass overmantel remained not only the height of luxury – it was expensive – but also a practical necessity, especially in large rooms, where it reflected and therefore substantially increased the amount of artificial and natural light.

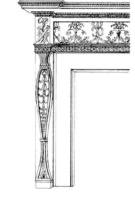

Above: *Bold profiles and high relief decoration typical of 1760s surrounds.*

Above: *By the late 1760s, relief had become lower and ornament more delicate.*

Below: *Pompeian and Etruscan motifs, c.1775.*

Below: *French-inspired, flowing Rococo lines, c.1790.*

Above: *A detail of a late 18th-century chimneypiece, showing typical Etruscan motifs on the frieze and* jambs. *Archaeological excavations in Greece fuelled the fashion for this style of Classical ornament.*

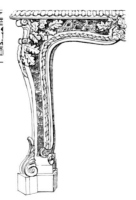

Right: *An elegant white marble fireplace from the end of the 19th century.*

The surrounding walls have been faux marbled to match the real marble slips.

AMERICAN FIREPLACES

The simplest of early North American fireplaces consisted of little more than plain wooden frames with mud or plaster infills. Primarily found in slave houses, they remained in use until the latter part of the 18th century. Not surprisingly, few have survived.

In the more substantial houses of the early settlers the fireplace was the social centre of the household, and therefore always received some decorative emphasis. However, the demands of cooking and the inclusion of features such as bake ovens and salt boxes made them very much working fixtures, and thus decoration and embellishments tended to be limited to simple carvings on jambs and lintels, dates and rustic motifs on wrought-iron firebacks, and patterned brickwork in the large open hearth.

Right: Located in one of the rooms of a Colonial house on Rhode Island, this fireplace has been restored to something close to its original condition and appearance: the softwood (pine) surround has been milk-painted in an earth colour and the joints of the stone hearth re-mortared. The pair of wrought iron andirons incorporate stands intended for warming jugs of wine. Hanging a picture over the mantel shelf was a typical means of decorating the wall above the fireplace in Colonial houses.

Left: Although located in a corner, the fireplace is the focal point of this bedroom in an 18th-century Colonial house. Grouping panelled cupboards (there is one on the wall above the mantel shelf), closets and doors around the fireplace, and painting them the same colour as the wooden fire-surround – as here – was common practice in houses of this period.

Toward the end of the 17th century, however, in houses of any size the kitchen and other living rooms gradually began to be separated. Where this was the case, sitting and drawing-room fireplaces, freed from the demands of cooking, became more refined and the decorative focal point that they already had been for some time on the other side of the Atlantic, in the British Isles and Europe.

Throughout the 18th century most chimney-pieces were inspired by the designs – largely Classical – that featured in the numerous pattern books imported from England and, to a lesser extent, Europe. High-quality marble fireplaces were invariably imported from Europe, as were Delft tiles (from The Netherlands) for fireplace slips. Wooden fire-surrounds, on the other hand, were often made up locally and given a wide

Above: *A fireplace from a Colonial house on Rhode Island with brass and iron andirons, poker and shovel.*

Right: *An example of a fireplace found in "middle-class" houses in New York in the mid-18th century.*

Left: *This mid-18th-century fireplace from a house in New York features imported Delft tile slips.*

Above: *The simplicity of style is typical of fireplaces in the "lesser rooms" of mid-18th-century houses.*

range of treatments, such as wood-graining and marbling, in imitation of more prestigious (and expensive) materials. The abundance of wood in large areas of the American colonies also promoted the widescale and extensive use of wall-panelling that, in many cases, looked like an extension or part of the chimneypiece itself.

The finest chimneypieces during the American Colonial period (1607–1780) had pilasters or mouldings surmounted by carvings of fruit and flowers, Aesop's and Biblical fables, or Classical motifs. It was also common practice to hang a picture on the panelling above the fire-surround, or to paint one – usually a landscape – directly on to a central panel.

Up until the end of the 18th century grates and stoves were rare – andirons being the normal accessory of the American wood-burning hearth. Andirons were imported in large numbers from England, but they were also made locally.

Above: *An elegant parlour chimney-piece in a house in Germantown, Philadelphia. It dates from 1764–7. While the slips and lintel are of a stridently veined marble, carving is restricted to the egg-and-dart moulding around them, and to the foliated consoles which support the moulded mantel shelf. Both the overmantel and the surround are "eared" – a fashionable embellishment of the time.*

Left: *From a house on Rhode Island, this mid-18th-century fireplace features grain-painted panelling, imported Delft tile slips and, in the hearth, a splendid pair of wrought-iron andirons with brass finials.*

Above: *A parlour chimney-piece, c.1758. in a house in Newport, Rhode Island. The* slips, *lintel and hearth projection have been faux marbled in paint.*

Above: *Another example of mid-18th-century marbling. The cost of importing real* marble from Europe made the painted version an attractive proposition.

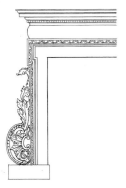

Above left: *Egg-and-dart mouldings, pulvinated frieze, Rococo-style brackets and capped dentilation, c.1740.*

Above middle: *Early 18th-century design, commonly used in hallways.*

Above right: *Bracketed surround, with carved dolphins on the lintel, c.1750.*

Left: *Carved floral motifs, c.1750.*

Above: *A dining room chimneypiece of 1761–2. It is distinguished by fine carving and a Chippendale-style pediment.*

Above: *This fireplace, from the great drawing room in Drayton Hall, Charleston, South Carolina, c.1740, reveals the popularity of English and European styles in the Southern Colonies. It was derived from William Kent's* Designs of Inigo Jones, *published in England in 1727. The family crest displayed on the overmantel was intended as much for a confirmation of status as decoration.*

Above left: *A carved and painted wooden fire-surround, with matching wall panelling (c.1790) from a house in Colchester, Connecticut. The fluted columns and broken pediment are the epitome of Classical design. The cracked and empty panel in the middle of the overmantel would have originally contained a painting – probably a landscape.*

Left: *This fireplace in Hunter House, Rhode Island (1758), has its picture panel intact, although it is not known whether the landscape was painted specifically for this overmantel.*

GRATES

Although wood remained the main source of fuel in North America until the 19th century, in the cities and towns of 18th-century Europe it was increasingly passed over in favour of coal, even in the grandest of houses where hitherto it had been thought rather vulgar to burn anything other than logs. Early in the period the coals were held in a fire basket, or dog grate, originally intended for wood. This was placed on a stone or marble hearth slab within the open brick arch of the (wide) hearth. However, it was soon discovered that coal required a smaller grate and hearth if it was to burn efficiently; also, that the grate had to be raised to draw the fire and collect the ash. Consequently, from the 1720s in newly built houses the fireplace opening was made smaller and cast-iron hob grates began to appear.

Unlike the free-standing dog grates, the new hob grates were fixed and took up the whole width of the new narrower fireplace. During the second half of the century they became universal in smaller houses and in the lesser rooms of mansions. Early hob grates were not particularly efficient, mainly because of the size of chimney flues. The problem was remedied in the 1790s by Sir Benjamin Thompson, Count von Rumford, who designed a hob grate with the basket further forward, so as to minimize the loss of heat up the chimney. It had canted sides to reflect heat into the room, and a narrower flue to improve the draw of the fire and reduce smokiness.

Left: *Design for a dog grate in the Gothic style by Thomas Chippendale, from* The Gentleman and Cabinet Maker's Director *(1762).*

Below: *Simple cast-iron hob grates such as the one shown here (c.1790) were usually embellished with fluting or chevrons.*

Above: *An engraving of a highly decorated register grate, taken from* The Builder's Magazine *of 1778. It would have occupied the entire hearth and had adjustable iron plates in the flue to regulate the draught.*

Below: *A late 18th-century, cast-iron register grate, incorporating a decorative plaque and framed by tiles of Flemish origin.*

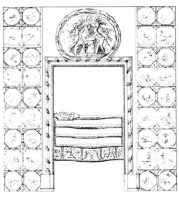

During the second half of the century, hob grates also became as important an element in the decorative effect of the fireplace as the surround, overmantel and cast-iron fireback. Typically they had urn-shaped sides and were decorated with Classical motifs along the front. Free-standing dog-grates, which remained a popular choice for the large hearths still found in the more important rooms of grander houses, were also increasingly ornamented. The finest examples were made of polished steel with applied and engraved Classical motifs, in the Adam style. Thomas Chippendale also designed dog grates in Rococo and Gothic styles. Where wood was still burnt, such as in North America and rural areas of Europe, andirons remained necessary, their ornamentation, as in the previous century, reflecting current styles and taste.

A further addition to the practical and decorative elements of the fireplace during the 18th century was the fender. Made of pierced metal – brass or steel – it was required to catch any coals falling from the new raised grates and prevent them from falling off the hearth and on to the carpet or wooden floor. Fenders were usually accompanied by a matching poker, tongs, shovel and brush, and a coal bucket, or purdonium. As in the late 17th century, painted chimney boards were used to cover the opening of the fireplace and reduce draughts during the summer months, although during the second half of the 18th century a few grates incorporated a metal shutter to close off the hearth. (In some households, when the fire was not in use, decorative fanned papers were arranged in the hearth instead of the shutter being closed or the chimney-board being put up.)

Above: *A late 18th-century hob grate augmented with a simple but stylish fireguard clipped onto its bars.*

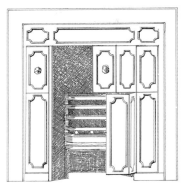

Above: *A very early Regency register grate sits within a handsome marble surround which turns at the corners on quarter columns.*

Left: *A late 18th-century illustration of a grate with shutters for closing the hearth when the fire was not lit.*

Above middle right: *An Adam-style basket or dog grate c. 1770.*

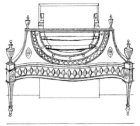

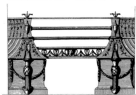

Above: *An illustration of a fine wrought-iron hob grate, taken from* The Builder's Magazine, *1778.*

Stoves and ranges

In the larger kitchens of grander houses, the old system of an open grate over which pots could be hung when cooking (which remained in poorer homes well into the 19th century) was gradually replaced by a fairly primitive cast-iron kitchen range, incorporating ovens and roasting spits. Some of the latter were fan-driven by jacks at the bottom of the flue. Wood- or coal-burning stoves, which were in the early stages of development, became increasingly common in Europe, Scandinavia and North America. In the case of the latter they appeared in some German and Dutch settlements quite early in the 18th century, but did not come into widespread use until much later, following the introduction of an improved design by Benjamin Franklin. In England, however, stoves were considered "vulgar". Blondel, for example, felt it was acceptable to have a stove in the dining room, but not in any other important room because "they could not but procure much dirtiness" – an opinion that would have been considered something of a luxury by those living in a colder climate.

Above and right: *Cast-iron stoves were available in Britain from the middle of the 18th century, but never caught on to the same extent as they did in Europe and North America.*

Left: *A very early cast-iron cooking range. First patented by Thomas Robinson in 1780, the basic design remained largely unaltered for over a hundred years. Unfortunately for the cook, early models were prone to going out unexpectedly.*

19th-Century Fireplaces

In Regency England (1811–20), fire-surrounds retained the relatively simple, rectilinear form of the classically-inspired models that had appeared toward the end of the 18th century. Typically, they consisted of flat jambs, or uprights, decorated with attenuated reeding, the latter repeated on a straight lintel. The jambs rose from squared base blocks, the corners were simple roundels, while the thin mantel shelf was often also reeded along its edge. As the period wore on, the jambs became wider and the shelf, sometimes supported by heavy scrolled brackets, gradually increased in depth and projected further at the sides; a development influenced by the fashion for displaying mantel clocks (some under a glass dome) and other functional or decorative objects, such as vases, spill holders and candlesticks.

Above and behind them, an overmantel mirror completed the picture in the smartest of Regency drawing rooms.

The finest surrounds were made of creamy-white statuary marble, although black, white and lightly veined gray marble were also fashionable. More extravagant examples sometimes incorporated porphyry or other rare, coloured marbles. However, for middle-class houses, and the less important rooms of grander houses, wooden replicas were produced. These were invariably painted, as in the previous century, usually to resemble marble, and often embellished with composition (a mixture of paper or wood pulp, whiting and glue, which was moulded into motifs and set rock hard – Egyptian motifs being much in vogue during the early 1820s).

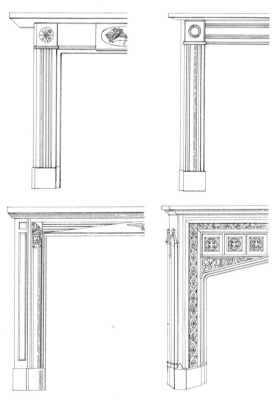

Clockwise from top left: Carved tablets were popular until 1825; Regency reeded jambs and corner roundels; A "Grecian" design c.1820;

Wider jambs and fleshy leaf forms typical of the 1830s; 1820s' Gothic revival; Egyptian motifs, popular until the 1820s.

A white marble surround with reeded decoration,

designed by Sir John Soane for his own house in 1812.

Above: *An illustration of a grand Egyptian ensemble, taken from Rudolf Ackermann's* Repository of Arts, Literature, Fashion Etc., *published in the early years of the 19th century.*

Right: *A carved wooden Regency fire-surround, painted to look like marble. The slips and lintel are also faux marbled, but in a more strident and colourful style.*

A black fossiliferous marble surround, with inset

Classical reliefs, designed by Sir John Soane in 1812.

A rather pretty Gothic revival surround of the

1830s. The brick arch and gas fire are from the 1920s.

Above: *A particularly fine example of an early 19th-century, English Regency chimneypiece, in the manner of Thomas Hope. The frieze has been carved with anthemion leaf decoration and is supported by flanking pairs of fluted Corinthian columns.*

Above: *A rather plain early 19th-century fireplace that displays the mimimum of applied or carved ornament. The surround has been faux marbled, and it frames a cast-iron, arch-topped register grate that has been black-leaded, rather than polished.*

Right: *A superb example of a statuary marble, Regency chimneypiece in the manner of Thomas Hope. The jambs feature profiled, inverted brackets and panels of anthemion beneath rosettes. The blockings are embellished with Medusa masks, and the running frieze has been carved with alternating Classical masks, foliate scrolls and anthemion.*

Above: *A statuary marble fireplace in an early 19th-century New York house.*

The slightly raised hearth is fairly typical of American fireplaces of this period.

Above: *Sited in one of the main drawing rooms of a large house in New York,*

this early 19th-century fireplace shows the influence of French Empire style.

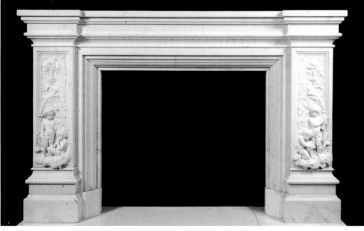

Left: *A painted wooden chimneypiece, c.1830s. This type of fireplace was consigned to the lesser rooms of grander houses.*

Above: *A William IV, statuary marble chimneypiece. In the centre of the arch-topped opening there is a pair of embracing putti.*

Left: *A grand, early 19th-century, William IV marble chimneypiece. Executed in the neo-Classical manner, its jambs are carved extensively with foliate scrolls and putti representing the liberal arts in deep relief. The frieze is carved with guilloche and supports a massive mantel shelf.*

Above: *An early 19th-century, French marble chimneypiece, with a serpentine-profile frieze. Reasonably large numbers of this style of surround were exported to Britain and North America during this period.*

Right: *A good quality, English marble chimneypiece in a restored 1820s house in London. The flanking busts on pillars lend an austere quality that has been partly offset by the elaborate Rococo-style gilt mirror overmantel.*

Above: *A substantial pale, veined marble chimneypiece from a house in King's Cross, in London. The heavy scrolled brackets and flat, wide jambs became increasingly popular in England during the 1830s.*

Above: *The flowing lines and extravagantly carved details of the Rococo-revival style became particularly fashionable in wealthier urban households from the late 1820s through to the early 1840s.*

NORTH AMERICAN FEDERAL AND EMPIRE

In North America the pattern-book designs of the Adam brothers proved the major influence in the transition from the colonial-style fireplace to the neo-Classical forms popular during the late-18th and first half of the 19th century. The fine marble chimneypieces imported from Europe, many featuring engaged columns supporting decorated entablatures, remained the preserve of the wealthy, as they had done earlier. Less expensive wooden fire-surrounds and overmantels were installed in smaller houses, some incorporating plain or coloured marble slips and, like the marble versions, a mythological scene on the central panel, together with applied moulded urns, garlands, swags, paterae and figures. The plainest fireplaces featured simple alternating patterns of goudgework.

Regardless of the basic material – marble or wood – by the 1830s such chimneypieces became bolder in style, and boasted Classical revival features such as Ionic or Tuscan columns and Greek key motifs (the latter particularly common in New York at this time), executed in black, white or gray marble. By around 1840, the fashion for intricate carving had waned to the extent that marble was often used just in slab form.

As far as the North American hearth was concerned, where logs were still burnt, cast-iron andirons continued to be used in lesser houses, whereas brass andirons, embellished with Classical urns or spherical finials were more common in grander houses. Cast-iron firebacks tended to feature neo-Classical patterns or the eagle motif. More progressive householders installed cast-iron liners instead, which were designed to radiate heat into the room. In addition, the Benjamin Franklin stove, which incorporated a grate with a liner and which had come into common use as early as 1785, remained a popular alternative – as did various types of hob grate (Bath stoves) imported from Britain.

Above: *A Classical, painted wooden English chimneypiece, c.1808. The Ionic columns support a dentillated entablature decorated with composition figures and swags-and-tails. The slips are marble.*

Left: *An imported, Classical-style fireplace in an early 19th-century house in Connecticut. The black and gold marble pillars are painted. The brick hearth has been restored.*

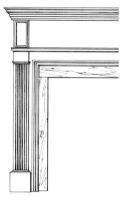

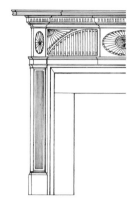

Left: *A chimneypiece from c.1808 with reeded wooden consoles, marble slips and a central plaque on the frieze depicting Bacchic figures on a chariot.*

Above left, middle and opposite: *Three typical neo-Classical fire-surrounds found in American Federal houses during the early years of the 19th century.*

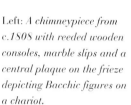

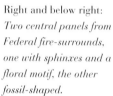

Right and below right: *Two central panels from Federal fire-surrounds, one with sphinxes and a floral motif, the other fossil-shaped.*

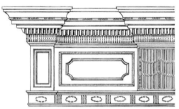

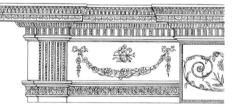

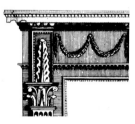

Top left, right and above: *Details showing applied motifs, dentil work and moulded panels; stucco swags; and composition mouldings.*

Right: *A Greek revival, Belgian, black marble fireplace from the 1860s.*

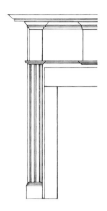

Right: *A substantial black marble chimneypiece, with brass andirons and fender in the hearth. Dating from the middle of the 19th century, this surround was installed in a secondary reception room of a large house.*

Below: *Two designs by William Pain, illustrating anthemion and diaper motifs cut along the frieze.*

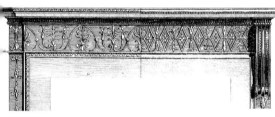

Left: *Installed in a mid-19th-century New York house, this is an English surround, with fossil marble slips and a recessed hearth.*

Above: *An English raised coal grate of brass and iron installed in a North American marble chimney-piece, c.1840s.*

VICTORIAN BRITAIN

In Victorian Britain(1837–1901) the fireplace, like interiors as a whole, appeared in a wide range of decorative styles, most of them period or revival as the inventive Victorians borrowed from and adapted the past. At various times, Baronial, Elizabethan, Queen Anne revival, Aesthetic, Arts and Crafts, Gothic and neo-Georgian styles, for example, were fashionable. However, some developments were common to most Victorian styles.

Firstly, in fashionable houses, fire-surrounds were often changed when rooms were redecorated in a new style. Traditionally, the finest examples were made of marble and, as before, replicas were available in wood for smaller homes and the secondary rooms of grander houses. Those made of inferior woods, such as pine, were painted, either plain or to resemble better materials, while better-quality hardwood surrounds were stained and varnished to bring out the natural figuring and grain of the wood. Later in the century, black or gray slate also became a less expensive and popular alternative to marble, which was becoming increasingly more expensive. However, the major development lay in the mass-production of cast-iron fire-surrounds and inserts which, as the foundries became increasingly skilled, gained in sophistication to the point where they were sometimes installed in important reception rooms, as well as in lesser rooms. While some were black-leaded others were painted, usually white, in a pastiche of marble.

Secondly, in the latter stages of the century, fire-surrounds generally became smaller, and the size was deliberately scaled to that of the room. The degree of ornamentation, as in previous centuries, also tended to be in proportion to the social importance of the room.

Thirdly, as the century wore on the weight and depth of the mantel shelf gradually increased in order to accommodate the display of an increasing array of *objets d'art* such as: clocks, vases, bowls, fans, candlesticks, busts, cameos, photographs, fossils, and all the other items the Victorians liked to collect and display. During the 1870s the chimney cloth, which first appeared in the 17th century, came back into fashion. Although it was originally intended to reduce smoke in the room, for the Victorians it was primarily another decorative feature.

Above: *A cast-iron fireplace, with tile slips, dating from the middle of the 19th century. Intended for one of the lesser rooms in the house, such as a secondary bedroom, it was painted white to simulate marble.*

Above: *A stripped pine fire-surround, with English delftware slips, typical of minor rooms around the mid-19th century. The cast-iron grate is decorated with floral motifs, possibly indicating a rural setting.*

Above: *A plain marble surround with a one-piece cast-iron insert providing a frame for the tiled slips. From a house in Glasgow, c.1892.*

Above: *An 1890s, three-tiered corner fireplace with picture-panel tile slips and a host of Victorian Classical and Romantic decorations.*

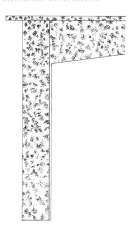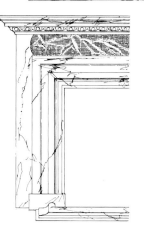

Above: *A late 19th-century English marble chimney-piece with a bronze-gilded mirror overmantel. The painted and gilded cast-iron insert is French.*

Left to right: *Cottage-style, painted wooden; Elaborate marble, for a dining room or library; Queen Anne revival by Richard Norman Shaw in the 1880s.*

A reaction to the "clutter" on the mantel shelf set in, particularly among the Aesthetic and Arts and Crafts movements, during the third quarter of the century. Not before, however, the development of increasingly complicated wooden overmantels, which usually incorporated a central mirror flanked by columns, side mirrors, and shelving for yet further displays. (The reduction in cost and the availability of plate glass resulted in the overmantel mirror – the preserve of the wealthy earlier in the century – replacing the painting or plaster panel in smaller houses.)

An increasingly wide range of painted and glazed ceramic tiles became available during the

Above left and right: *Two chimneypieces from a late 19th-century Arts and Crafts house in London. Both reflect the Victorian passion for drawing on past styles and designs for inspiration, and adapting them for their own purposes. Here, Classical-revival dominates the decorative elements, notably in the fluted columns and brackets, swags-and-chains, rows of arches and, in the example on the right, a broken pediment.*

Left: *A polished mahogany fire-surround with matching wooden overmantel. Dating from the third quarter of the 19th century, its bold Baronial style was much in vogue in larger houses during this period. The level of detailing is exceptional, notably in the overmantel, where carved niches, turned and fluted columns, a richly carved foliate frieze and middle panel bearing a coat-of-arms, surround a picture panel incorporating a seascape.*

second half of the century. Attractive, durable and easy to clean, they became very popular, initially in large houses but eventually, when the price dropped as a result of mass-production, throughout the rest of the housing stock. Apart from being fixed into the sides of the cast-iron register grate, they were also used to line the surface of hoods designed to draw smoke up and away from the room.

Throughout the period the impedimenta of the hearth – pokers, tongs, shovels, brushes and coal scuttles – became increasingly elaborate, as did fenders or fireguards, which grew correspondingly decorative.

Above: *A mid-19th-century, plain cast-iron, standard register grate.*

Above: *Two late 19th-century register grates from the William Owen foundry.*

Above: *A late 1850s, one-piece cast-iron fireplace. The floral motifs on the jambs and frieze were a typical embellishment of the period. The purchaser of such a fireplace would have almost certainly been given a choice as to the colour and pattern of the tiled slips flanking the grate.*

Right: *Some of Pryke and Palmer's pictoral ceramic tiles. Available individually or in panels, they became a popular addition to the fireplace during the second half of the 19th century.*

Above: *A Pryke and Palmer register grate from their catalogue of 1896.*

Above: *This wooden fire-surround in a Gothic revival house has been given a faux stone finish.*

Above right: *A design for a Gothic, dressed stone fire-place featuring an integral stone curb.*

Below: *A particularly hand-some fireplace c. 1894, lined with Italianate majoli-ca tiles and fitted with a*

substantial dog grate. The turned and carved wooden surround has been executed to a very high standard.

Left: *Classical motifs, over-mantel with mirror and elaborately tiled slips are typical of fireplaces found in grander houses during the 1890s Georgian revival.*

Right (detail): *A Victorian cast-iron fireplace – the frieze is decorated with swags and roundels.*

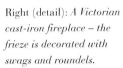

Above: *A Victorian bedroom fireplace with patterned tile slips and a copper canopy emblazoned with a sunburst.*

Left: *An elaborate, mid-19th-century, Gothic revival wooden and plaster fire-surround. The inset panels of the overmantel are from an earlier period (probably 17th-century Dutch). Much of the carved woodwork is stained mahogany; gold metallic paint and a bronze antiquing glaze has been applied to the plaster and carvings.*

Above (detail): *An elaborate stone, Gothic revival chimneypiece (c. 1860) from one of the main reception rooms* in Strawberry Hill, Middlesex, England. The undercutting of the floral frieze is a tour de force.

Above: *A mass-produced cast-iron chimneypiece with a painted oak grain finish made by the Carron Company.*

AMERICAN "VICTORIAN" FIREPLACES

During the Victorian period in the United States, which, in terms of many aspects of decorative style, stretched up to 1910, the fireplace assumed a position of tremendous importance. Mary Gay Humphreys, the prolific writer on household taste, described it thus: "The fireplace is really the domestic altar, the true rallying point of the household" – a view largely explained by the hardships of having to face severely cold winters in a wooden house. Even after the advent of the stove, at the end of the 18th century, and the introduction of central heating in larger houses during the latter part of the 19th century, the fireplace retained both its decorative and symbolic importance. Moreover many people thought that stoves, which eliminated draughts and made rooms stuffy, were also unhealthy. Combined with the fact that an open fire was a sign of wealth – the fuel was more expensive, and servants were required to tend to the fire – it is hardly surprising that the fireplace remained "the domestic altar" and was not rendered obsolete.

In America, as in Britain, a wide range of revival styles proved popular and fashionable throughout the period. The most stylish examples

Above: *An 1870s American Victorian fireplace with wooden surround and pictoral tile slips.*

Above: *An 1840s Italian marble fireplace, installed in the parlour of a house in Vicksburg, Mississippi.*

Left: *A marbled chimney-piece in the formal parlour of a house in Hannibal Missouri, c.1870s.*

Below: *An 1880–90s neo-Classical fireplace (left), and an Arts and Crafts example from the same period.*

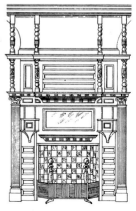

of the 1850s and 1860s were the marble Rococo-revival and marble or wooden Renaissance-revival designs; the latter were embellished with incised decoration. Many of these chimneypieces were imported from Europe, particularly from Italy, although some were made in the United States. Neo-Classical chimneypieces, in marble, slate and wood and of almost Grecian simplicity, were also popular, especially in Shingle-style houses. Queen Anne styles were fashionable during the 1870s and 1880s and Arts and Crafts-inspired fireplaces appeared during the latter part of the 19th century.

The popularity of historical-revival styles in the United States during the last quarter of the 19th century was in no small part inspired by architects, such as Richard Morris Hunt, of the Beaux Arts Movement. Having travelled to Europe to study architecture at the École des Beaux Arts in Paris, they returned to promote the use of advanced technology for the construction of houses, but combined with historically derived architectural styles and details. They were to remain influential up until the end of the 1920s.

All styles held pride of place in the living-halls of later Victorian houses, and in some rooms the

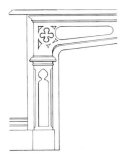

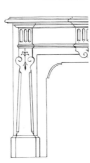

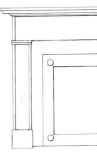
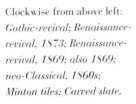

Below: *A late-19th-century wooden chimneypiece, with tiles, in relief, depicting hunting scenes. There is a cover for closing the grate during the summer months.*

Clockwise from above left: *Gothic-revival; Renaissance-revival, 1873; Renaissance-revival, 1869; also 1869; neo-Classical, 1860s; Minton tiles; Carved slate.*

Below left: *A Queen Anne fireplace from the 1870s or 1880s, with a wooden over-mantel and brick surround.*

Below right: *A Queen Anne brick fireplace of 1881, incorporating a soapstone mantel shelf.*

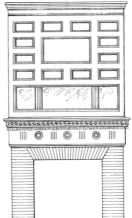

Right: *An ornate, late Victorian fireplace, with numerous painted built-in cupboards and niches, a wealth of gilding, and contrasting marble slips and lintel. The standard of craftsmanship, particularly as far as the joinery is concerned, is exceptionally high and reflects the influence of the Arts and Crafts Movement.*

Above (detail): *The patterned tile slips and frieze of a American Victorian wooden chimneypiece.*

Below: *An elaborately carved, Rococo-revival chimneypiece, installed in a formal reception room of a house in New York during the second half of the 19th century.*

Below: *An American Victorian Renaissance-revival fireplace, with flanking double columns in the jambs and, unusually, dogs' heads in the spandrels of the arched surround.*

notion of a cosy hearth and an open fire was augmented by a complex ensemble of overmantels, display shelves for works of art, decorative panels, scenic pictorial slip tiles and built-in seats, which combined to reinforce the fireplace as the focal point of the room.

The fireplace was also the focal point in the enormous halls and galleries of mansions built in the François Premier style during the Beaux Arts period in last quarter of the century. They could not be described, however, as cosy, like many of the fireplaces in ordinary homes. With the advent of central heating they were freed from function, and remained purely symbolic or ornamental (and designed to impress visitors). Some featured huge limestone hoods that stretched to the ceiling, and were tall enough to walk into. Others, such as those in the Italian Renaissance-revival style were framed by stone or marble surrounds embellished with elaborate Classical carving.

Above: *A late-19th-century, American Tudor-revival fireplace. Embellishments* *include attenuated columns, quatrefoil patterns, and floral and foliate motifs.*

Above: *An incredibly ornate American Beaux Arts fireplace from the late-19th century. A tabernacle of carved mahogany encloses contrasting coloured and patterned marbles, the whole composition and the various decorative motifs being a hybrid of French and Italian Renaissance designs.*

Right: *A French Classical-revival surround in a late Victorian American house.*

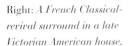

Similarly, Spanish-revival fireplaces made an impressive sight, with their rows of stone or wood carvings on the chimney-breast.

More discreet models, such as those in the French Classical-revival style were smaller, and often comprised a wooden frame of delicate Rococo leaf carving or a shallow mantel shelf with Louis XVI columnar supports. Similarly, Georgian-revival surrounds were simply marked by elements of a single Classical order in marble or wood, with reeded or plain columns. These simpler chimneypieces of the latter Beaux Arts period were to remain popular well into the 20th century. Less flamboyant than the monumental examples which were popular earlier in the period and in the largest of houses, they marked a transitional stage in the gradual simplification of the fireplace that was to result in the far less imposing fire-surrounds of the First World War and beyond.

Right: *An American, Tudor-revival stone fireplace from the last quarter of the 19th century. The four-centred arch and carved spandrels are typical of the style. The stained and polished linefold wall panelling add period character.*

Below: *A large and imposing American Beaux Arts chimneypiece of 1883, incorporating a mirrored overmantel. The design is a rather liberal interpretation of Italian Renaissance style.*

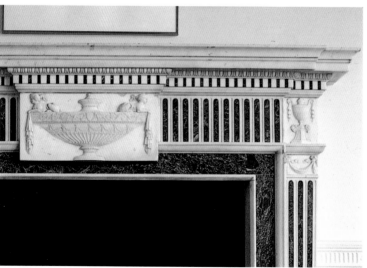

Above: *A François Premier style fireplace of unusual proportions, in Issac Fletcher House, New York. A transitional style, François Premier linked French Gothic traditions with those of the Renaissance. The Gothic is reflected in the wide pointed arch surround (bearing Gothic tracery) framing the amber marble facing. The flanking Corinthian columns and the carvings in the spandrels are closely associated with the Italian Renaissance.*

Left (detail): *A 19th-century Classical fireplace, showing urns on the central plaque and top of the pilaster.*

Left: *An "eared" wooden chimneypiece from the middle of the 19th century. Dentil mouldings and floral swags-and-tails on the over-mantel frieze are typical Classical details. The blue and white, geometric patterned tiles are, however, quite unusual. While the surround itself is painted off-white to resemble marble, the fender enclosing the tiled hearth is real marble.*

Below left: *A Victorian cast-iron grate flanked by blue and white English Delft tiles decorated with leaping horsemen. The tiles are probably of an earlier date than the grate, although they could be Victorian "reproductions".*

Below right: *Detail of a small cast-iron, Victorian grate. The brass hood can be opened or closed in order to adjust the updraught. The original clay fireback, despite the discolouration, cracking and crazing is in remarkably good condition for its age.*

Above: *A late Victorian, slab marble chimneypiece with a cast-iron insert and raised grate. While marble* remained the first choice for better quality surrounds, scagliola and other compos- *ite materials were also used.*

Above: *A particularly fine example of a 19th-century English chimneypiece. Made of statuary marble it is* styled in the manner of *Thomas Hope, and would have been used in a grand reception room.*

Right: *A magnificant, mid-19th-century, neo-Gothic chimneypiece. Carved from limestone, it was originally installed in Rivermead House, Sunbury, by Sir James Lewis Knight-Bruce. The shield over the middle of the triple-arch opening bears his coat-of-arms.*

Left: *A late-19th-century, cast-iron chimneypiece, painted white. The ash drawer at the base of the grate is faced with a decorative ceramic tile.*

Above: *A white faux marbled wooden surround that has real marble slips and lintel. This fireplace dates from the last quarter of the 19th century.*

Above: *A late-19th-century painted wooden surround. The simple Classical style is embellished with the minimum of decoration – largely confined to the egg-and-dart moulding around the marble tile slips. The brass fire screen is an elegant example of a type usually employed in a formal sitting or drawing room.*

Above: *A similar surround to the one shown above left. Wooden surrounds of this period were invariably made of pine and painted on site. The practice of stripping off the paint and staining and varnishing the pine is a fashion of the late 20th century, and not entirely appropriate for the majority of urban settings.*

ARTS AND CRAFTS MOVEMENT

During the 19th century numerous decorative styles of fireplace were fashionable at various points in time. Surrounds in the Rococo revival, Renaissance revival (French and Italian), neo-Classical (Italian and Greek), and Gothic revival styles came and went, their forms broadly based on those of earlier centuries. Of special note were the designs associated with the Aesthetic and Arts and Crafts, and the Art Nouveau, movements during the late 19th century.

In their search for the traditional values of pre-mass-production craftsmanship and hearth and home, members of the Arts and Crafts Movement placed special emphasis on the fireplace. Although sometimes inspired by motifs of the Middle Ages, the style they created was totally original. The consequences of this were varied: the most significant being a revival of the inglenook, which in largest houses were often massive in scale. Other, grander, examples resembled enormous Renaissance chimney breasts, while the most exotic were finely detailed Islamic or Chinese set-pieces. The simplest featured plain wooden surrounds on stone or brick chimney breasts, with additional wooden shelving above

Above: *A late-19th-century, American Arts and Crafts fireplace. The wooden surround, decorated with* *floral motifs on the frieze and jambs, frames a carved marble insert with a Moorish arch.*

Left: *A late-19th-century Arts and Crafts fireplace. The plain surround is made of slate. The cast-iron grate is polished, rather than blacked, while the hood above is decorated with Islamic-inspired fretwork.*

Above: *A brick chimney breast designed in 1859 by Philip Webb for the Red House, in Bexleyheath, near London. The cast-iron grate is flanked by English delft tiles, and topped by an adjustable brass hood.*

the mantel shelf for displaying blue and white china and other ceramics. Overmantels were a prominent feature of Arts and Crafts chimney-pieces, and were usually painted to co-ordinate with the colour of the surrounding walls, or ebonized to match the fashionable furniture of leading designers, such as E.W. Godwin.

Pictorial tiled slips were also a common feature of Arts and Crafts' inspired fireplaces, and leading designers of the Movement collaborated with manufacturers to produce some exquisite examples, notably: Walter Crane's tiles, produced by Minton in England and the American Encaustic

Tiling Company in the United States; the English ceramicist, William de Morgan's exclusive designs derived from Oriental patterns, and various examples based on the illustrations of English artist, Kate Greenaway.

Typical motifs, on both tiles and surrounds, included subjects from "Olde England", such as St George and the Dragon, while hob grates, dog grates and andirons – the latter revived as they encouraged the traditional burning of logs, rather than coal – were fashioned with similar motifs. Medieval-style jug and bottle warmers were even incorporated into some of the designs.

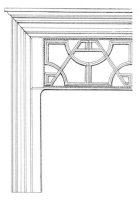

Above left to right: *Two carved wooden surrounds in the Aesthetic style; A carved walnut surround, dated 1875, by H. L. and W. H. Fry; An American, relief-tiled surround of 1896, by H. C. Mercer.*

Right: *Contrasting marbles and "Pre-Raphaelite-style" tiles dominate this early Arts and Crafts fireplace. On the hearth is a set of brass fire irons; the shovel and tongs resting on the brass andirons are purely ornamental.*

Left: *An Arts and Crafts fireplace of 1870, by Richard Norman Shaw. The* great carved corbels support the mantel shelf and frame the richly decorated recess.

ART NOUVEAU MOVEMENT

The influence of the Arts and Crafts Movement extended up until the end of the first quarter of the 20th century (see the following chapter, page 68), while Art Nouveau designs for fireplaces, which began to appear in the late 1880s, had a shorter, though significant, shelf-life. And, unlike Arts and Crafts' fireplaces, Art Nouveau designs were fully compatible with the mass-production of the late 19th century.

Typical fireplaces, such as those designed by Charles Rennie Mackintosh, incorporated shelving and cupboards and tended to repeat the forms of the new built-in furniture, while coloured glass mosaics around the grate set off colours used elsewhere in the room. Many Art Nouveau fire-surrounds were wooden, either painted or stained,

and incorporated the elongated curved forms and stylized plant shapes characteristic of the style. Marble, or faux marble, was also used, often in an exuberant manner, some of the most elaborate examples featuring sculptured caryatids with flowing hair. However, the most organic or "natural" forms appeared on the mass-produced, cast-iron fire-surrounds (which were usually black-leaded, rather than painted). Visually striking beaten copper surrounds (or components), were also quite common, particularly in the work of Scottish designer, George Walton. As with Arts and Crafts' fireplaces, a huge range of ceramic tiles appeared, produced in conjunction with designers, by companies such as Pilkington and Doulton in Britain, and the Encaustic Tiling Company in the United States.

Above: *A white-painted, cast-iron, Art Nouveau fireplace, c.1890s. The sculptural plant forms, typical of the style, are augmented with a pair of owls.*

Above: *Designed by C.R. Mackintosh in 1902–3, the drawing room fireplace at Hill House, in Helensburgh, Scotland, features ovals of coloured and mirror glass set in a mosaic surround.*

Right: *The main bedroom fireplace at Hill House, also by Mackintosh. The Art Nouveau motifs are executed in a palette of pink and mauve and subtly contrast with the polished cast-iron.*

GRATES

By the beginning of the 19th century the dog grate had been superseded by the more efficient enclosed hob grate. Hob grates were elegant in appearance, and became very fashionable (see 18th-Century Fireplaces, pages 37–8) but they proved to be inefficient and were soon replaced by the new cast-iron, register grate.

The register grate incorporated a damper to control the supply of air to the fire, and was supplemented with an additional damper in the throat of the chimney. Cast in one piece and forming the inner frame and back of the hearth, the register grate was set as an insert within the fire-surround. The register grate was more efficient than the hob grate and soon became very popular, especially in cities and towns, as early as the 1820s. Like the dog grate and hob grate, the register grate was complemented by a fender or fireguard and an ever-increasing array of fireplace accessories – pokers, tongs, brushes, coal scuttles and so on.

While dog grates – sometimes with brass ornamentation – continued to be used in large open fireplaces, such as were still found in the entrance halls of grand houses, the mass-produced, arch-topped, built-in register grate became virtually universal in town houses. It provided a degree of control over the strength of the draught, and could be used with or without a decorative surround. Many examples also featured an oval plate at the back which could be closed when the fire was not in use to prevent soot from falling from the chimney, and all but the simplest versions, as

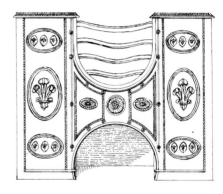

Left: *A steel grate with gilt mounts, from Rudolf Ackermann's early 19th-century* Repository of Arts, Literature, Fashions Etc.

Above: *An illustration of a handsome, free-standing grate of 1820, styled and decorated in the bold neo-Classical manner.*

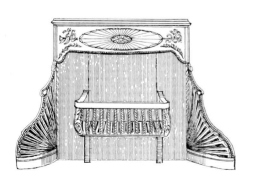

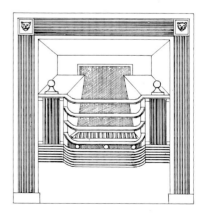

Above: *An ornately decorated Franklin stove, c.1785. The cast-iron back, or liner,* *behind the grate was designed to radiate heat into the room.*

Above: *"A Convex Reed Elliptic Register Stove, with Bright framed Fire, Double* *Rail, Balls, Bright Heads, Bevil Cheeks, falling Back, and Valve", (1811).*

Left: *A cast-iron hob grate, c.1820–30s. The gently curving fire-bars, with three balls, reflect chair-back designs of the period.*

Right: *A tiled register grate, suitable for a small town house, from Pryke and Palmer's 1896 catalogue.*

Right: *Three Victorian dog grates from the Carron Company. Mass-produced in cast iron, they were designed to burn coal. The best examples, intended for grander houses, featured brass ornamentation.*

Right: *A selection of turn of the century grates in the Art Nouveau style. The one on the left incorporates doors. The example in the middle is craftsman-made in wrought copper. The one on the right features an English "Derby" gas fire with artificial coals.*

Left: *Two American Victorian fireplace heaters. By pushing back the doors, the one on the right could be turned into an open grate.*

Right: *A late 19th-century gas fire, with cast-iron casing and asbestos elements.*

might be found in servant's quarters, were embellished with built-in tiled panels or slips. Gas fires became available late in the 19th century, and had the obvious advantages of: no coals to carry and light every day; no ashes to rake and dispose of, and no chimneys to sweep. However, the disadvantages – expensive to run, a tendency to blow out, and an unreliable supply of gas – carried greater weight until the advent of technical improvements in the 20th century.

Kitchen fireplaces

The built-in range, made from cast-iron and fuelled by coal, became the heart of the Victorian kitchen. Of the two basic types, the open grate and the enclosed grate, the latter became the most popular, primarily because pots and pans stayed cleaner and lasted longer when heated on top of a cast-iron plate rather than over an open fire. Among the other advantages of the enclosed range were its ability to maintain a fire overnight, its incorporation of both a water boiler and an oven (or two), and its relatively clean and economic fuel consumption.

Like the gas fire, the gas stove became available toward the end of the 19th century. However, town gas was not always available and the gas stove did not become widespread until the 20th century.

Above: *An end of century, cast-iron range in a house in Glasgow.*

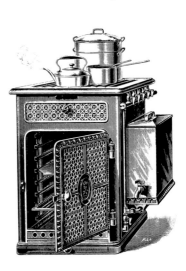

Above: *A cast-iron range, c.1890, with two ovens a semi-enclosed* grate, and two double-cone ventilators above a plate rack.

Left: *A built-in cast-iron range of the type found in many larger American Victorian homes from the 1870s onward. Although sophisticated for their day, only a few ranges have survived in the face of modern technology.*

Right: *A late 19th-century gas oven from the Carron Company. It incorporates a single oven, a grill, and an additional copper boiler for heating water.*

20th-Century Fireplaces

A variety of fireplace styles were fashionable in Edwardian Britain during the early years of the 20th century. In rural areas, for example, the Baronial or Tudor look was popular, especially in entrance halls, and the inglenook, which had been revived by the Arts and Crafts Movement in the latter part of the 19th century, remained a favoured method of providing draught-free seats around the fireplace. The Tudor style was also considered appropriate for dining or billiard rooms and libraries, especially if augmented with a curb of faïence, copper, brass or iron. Many fireplaces incorporated small shelves for the display of ornaments or books. Overmantels of the period came in painted pine, fumed and wax-polished oak, polished mahogany or walnut.

In town houses, designs derived from Art Nouveau models of the previous century also proved popular, as were copies of Queen Anne and Georgian styles, the latter often Adamesque in appearance, especially when situated in drawing rooms. Copies of Louis XV or XVI chimneypieces appeared in many large houses, either the earlier and more curvaceously scrolled models, or the strictly rectangular variety which stood proud of the chimney breast and featured a broad mantel shelf for displaying objects such as a clock or pieces of porcelain.

As in previous centuries, materials ranged from stone or marble, in the main reception rooms and bedrooms of grander houses, to enamelled slate (ornamented to look like inlaid marble) and wood in smaller houses. Wooden fireplaces were usually pine and often painted matte Georgian green or gloss white. There was also a greater use of glazed tiles, the most popular varieties came in plain colours with metallic glazes, while some had enriched borders.

Above: *An "artistic" fire-place, suitable for a bedroom. It has an adjust-able canopy that can be closed to reduce draughts.*

Above: *An Edwardian fire-place in a "Tudor" panelled setting. The marble archi-trave frames tiled cheeks,* which would have helped to throw heat into the room. The dog grate is of a type found in grander houses.

Right: *The surround and the semi-circular curb are in plain glazed faïence (tin-glazed earthenware).*

Above: *An unusual Gothic-style fireplace. The surround is fumed oak, and frames* *marble slips and Dutch-tile cheeks. The curb and canopy are copper.*

Above: *A retrogressive design, featuring tiles set in a pine mantel, supplied* *ready for painting. The over-mantel could be painted pine or polished walnut.*

Above: *A bedroom fireplace with a typically deep frieze containing a central swag-and-tail decorated panel.*

Right: *A painted cast-iron Edwardian chimneypiece with a "Tudor" hearth.*

REVIVAL STYLES

By the 1920s and 1930s a variety of revival styles were still being produced. However, they were usually simplified and sometimes installed in interiors that bore no relation to the original period. Popular fireplace designs included Adam style and Arts and Crafts – inglenooks being fairly common in Tudorbethan-style houses. The Arts and Crafts influence could also be seen in beaten brass and pewter curbs, pokers, tongs, brushes and purdonium. Such accessories were, of course, irrelevant where gas or electric fires were installed. Technical advances, including less expensive and more reliable supplies of gas and electricity, made them an increasingly popular alternative to coal or wood during the 1930s. Gas and electric fires were also used in the lesser rooms of larger houses to supplement central heating systems.

The attraction of a "real" fire, however, struck a chord with most people – Belling's coal-effect fires, introduced in 1921, and Berry's Magicoal electric fires proved to be very popular, as are their improved versions today.

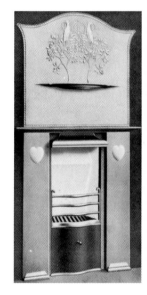

Left: *An early 19th-century, Georgian-style fireplace, featuring detailing in the Adam manner. Typically Edwardian is the treatment of the plain tiling with an enriched border. The integral grate is lined with firebricks.*

Right: *A simple, but finely proportioned cast-iron fireplace, with tall overmantel, reflecting the influence of the Arts and Crafts Movement during the first decade of the 20th century.*

Above: *A free-standing dog grate and cast-iron fireback, sits within a brick hearth and is framed by a blue marble surround.*

Right: *A white painted, cast-iron bedroom fireplace. The raised grate is flanked by Arts and Crafts style tiled cheeks.*

Above: *An Adamesque Edwardian fireplace, intended for a drawing room. The surround and overmantel are white painted pine.*

Right: *A "Queen Anne" style chimneypiece of 1906. The little shelves and glazed cupboards for displaying china and knick-knacks are typically Edwardian.*

Above: *A Berry "Magicoal" electric fire, from the early 1920s. Coal-effect fires such as this were first introduced by Belling in 1921.*

Left: *A 20th-century revival of a 16th-century fireplace featuring stop-chamfered jambs, a free-standing fire basket and a decorative iron fireback.*

MODERNIST AND ART DECO

Fireplaces remained fashionable in many homes on both sides of the Atlantic during the first half of the 20th century, although they were not incorporated into some of the new houses designed by Modernist architects. Where fireplaces were included they often remained the focal point of the room, although their architectural form was greatly simplified. In the United States such simplicity did not mean, however, loss of scale or visual impact. For example, the abstract compositions of Frank Lloyd Wright, built of rugged stonework, often extended across an entire wall in a series of horizontal bands.

Architects and designers working in the Art Deco style during the 1920s and 1930s produced fireplaces that displayed understated, simple clean lines and smooth planes. However, they were often striking in appearance, having either brilliantly reflective (chrome), lacquered (wood) or glazed (tiled) surfaces typical of a style that combined the reductivist aesthetic of Modernism with the European tradition of a rich and high-quality finish; the archetypal Art Deco fireplace being the chrome, wall-mounted electric fire.

Less grand examples of the Modernist fireplace made during the 1930s consisted of a plain stone surround set flush against the wall, sometimes with a tile infill. (In the late 1930s flint or stone became a popular replacement for tiles.) Panels of metal or stone were also set into the chimney breast above the surround as part of

Left: The asymmetrical mantel shelf, mottled tiles with contrasting inserts, and Art Deco electric fire, are typical of the 1930s.

Below: A highly styled Art Deco fireplace, c.1936, in a house in Florida. British Art Deco was more constrained by reference to the past.

Left: A very unusual Art Deco mirror-glass fire-surround from the 1940s. The observation that Art Deco was "domesticated cubism" *is amply borne out here, as is the belief among practitioners of the style that art and mass production were not mutually exclusive.*

asymmetrical compositions, while bookcases were often lined up on either side and recessed spaces provided for the storage of wood.

Other examples, both Modernist and Art Deco, consisted of just a rectangular opening, sometimes with a chromed edging, and a hearth of polished marble or stone. In Britain, brick hearths and chimney breasts, without ornamentation, were also in vogue, and were usually accompanied by a decorative iron fire basket or fire dogs. In the English suburbs, tiled surrounds were commonplace in the 1930s, usually pale green, beige or buff in colour, sometimes framed in wood and often stepped or asymmetrical in outline. Other features associated with Modernist and Art Deco fireplaces included, for example,

illuminated niches in the chimney breast for displaying *objets d'art*, hearths recessed some distance above the level of the floor, and fire-surrounds made from stainless steel or opaque or coloured glass.

In the 1950s the heat-saving device of a free-standing fire with a fluepipe connected directly to the chimney became popular in small houses, particularly in the United States, while in California, designers such as Richard Neutra often divided large open living spaces with a fireplace – its surface sometimes crazy-paved. During this period Modernists were also using metal, such as copper-louvered vents, as a means of concealing the fire and as a decorative feature in its own right.

Right: *A simple yet majestic Modernist fireplace in a house in California. Designed by Rudolph Schindler in 1922, it has a tall copper canopy or hood, which features subtle gradations of colour caused by a combination of oxidization and exposure to heat during manufacture and use. The employment of materials such as copper in this manner was pioneered by Adolf Loos in pre-1914 Vienna, where Schindler began his career.*

Left: *The stone chimney and hearth, c.1935, are built like an external wall in Frank Lloyd Wright's house, Falling-water, in Bear Run, Pennsylvania.*

Right: *Typical of the "Contemporary" style of the 1950s, this "crazy-paved" fireplace is used to divide the open living area of a house in California designed by Richard Neutra.*

Left: *Asymmetrical stepping, mottled tiles and wooden framing are typical of 1930s fireplaces – as is an illuminated wall niche. The wooden seats flanking the hearth double up as fuel bins, and are a faint echo of seating in the Jacobethan inglenook fireplace.*

Right: *While the style of this 1930s surround is 18th century, the stepped mirror with border decoration is very much contemporary.*

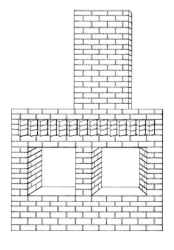

Above left: *Copper louvred vents conceal an electric heater, in this Modernist "fireplace" designed by Russell Wright.*

Above right: *The surround and hearth are stainless steel, the fire electric, in the room of a house in Poole, Dorset, c.1932.*

Left: *An illustration for a post-modern brick fireplace with raised twin openings – one for the hearth; one for storing fuel.*

Right: *Again, post-modern, a throwback to the medieval open hearth – the grate, ingeniously, is made from an old gearwheel.*

POST-MODERN

However, by the beginning of the second half of the 20th century – the Post-Modern period – the traditional decorative fireplace began to return to favour. While some Modernist innovations, such as free-standing island fireplaces, and fires fitted with hoods and stovepipes, have remained popular, period or revival styles have been much in demand. Original fireplaces, either whole or in part, have been salvaged, repaired or restored, and numerous companies (see the Directory, pages 122–4) have produced a wide range of reproductions in marble, stone, wood, plaster and fibreglass. This desire to restore or install period fireplaces, original or reproduction, has no doubt been given impetus by the development of authentic-looking, imitation coal and log fires fuelled by gas. Over and above all that, however, it reflects a recognition of the limitations of central heating which, despite its efficiency, deprives the householder of an almost primal need, that is, a focal point for warmth and light, around which one can gather in the main living room of the home.

Above: *A 1970s Classical chimneypiece with marble slips.*

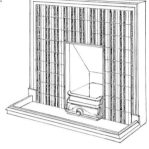

Above: *1950s Regency stripe tiles, walnut surround and stainless steel grate.*

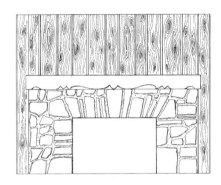

Above: *1970s "ranch look" – rough stone fireplace and pine surround.*

Left: *An imposing post-modern fireplace with engaged columns. Designed in 1980 by John Outram for the library of a house in Sussex, England.*

Above: *A late 1980s neo-Renaissance hooded fireplace, by Robert Adam. The moulded consoles with lions' feet revive a largely forgotten Classical form.*

GRATES, GAS AND ELECTRIC FIRES

Where logs were still burnt, dog-grates remained in use, especially in the halls or dining rooms of grander houses. Where Adam-style fireplaces were installed, grates were typically polished steel or black-leaded cast-iron, and accompanied by a pierced steel fender. However, one of the main concerns at this time was the need to reduce fuel (coal) consumption while maintaining or increasing the output of heat. As a result the cheeks of many fireplaces were made from fire-brick, and splayed at the sides, with the back sloping forward, in order to project more heat into the room. The splayed sides also reduced the size of the grate, and therefore the amount of fuel. Some grates were ventilated directly from outside, the fire thus not drawing a cold draught across the room.

Gas fires also became more efficient with the introduction of clay elements. However, they remained rather obtrusive, as did anthracite stoves, which appeared in the first decade of the 20th century and were able to burn through the night because they had a regulator controlling the rate of burning. Electric fires were also slightly improved. However, they remained particularly expensive to run, and were inadequate for heating larger rooms.

Right: *A Berry "Magicoal" electric fire. It was turned on and off by a foot switch.*

Below right: *A two-unit gas fire with bronze-lustre finish, set into an onyx surround – available from Bratt, Colbran and Company in 1934.*

Far left: *An Edwardian gas fire incorporating clay elements and a ring on top for a kettle.*

Left: *An Edwardian anthracite stove, with a feed door at the top and a regulator to control the rate of burning.*

Above: *An Edwardian interpretation of an 18th-century register grate, from the Carron Company.*

Above right: *A 1920s Classical surround, with marble slips and cheeks enclosing an electric fire.*

Stoves and ranges

In the kitchen the traditional coal-fired range had already become highly efficient by the end of the Victorian era. However, during the first quarter of the 20th century they were made easier to maintain: being set in tiles and given tiled backs and enamelled finishes. Despite these improvements they still required regular black-leading – a dirty and unpleasant job. Consequently, gas stoves became an increasingly attractive alternative, being easier to clean and far safer than the prototypes of the previous century. Electric stoves, on the other hand were still expensive to run and relatively inefficient.

In the United States wood-burning stoves were gradually supplanted by coal-burning versions and, eventually, gas-fired models. The new coal-burning types were squarer and lower than their Victorian predecessors, and featured symmetrical arrangements of between four to eight burners. Made of cast-iron, fashionable models were moulded into elaborate patterns of lattice-work, grape vines and various Neo-Classical details. Nickel mounts, hinges and door panels often provided additional ornamentation. Gas and electric stoves, which proved a great success in the United States quite early in the century, were of increasingly compact design and had easy-to-clean enamelled surfaces. Most featured far less decorative metal-work than the coal- or wood-burning alternatives.

By the 1920s and 1930s gas and electric stoves had come down in price. Gas remained notably cheaper than electricity, particularly in Britain, and offered greater control for cooking; the first thermostatic gas oven having appeared in 1923. Designs were also more advanced in the United States than Britain.

Developments in the design of cooking facilities during the second half of the century have mainly consisted of improvements to hobs (cooktops) and ovens, the popular combination of gas and electricity (usually a gas hob and an electric oven) to improve efficiency, and an increased minimalism – appliances being ever-more streamlined and unobtrusive. The only variations on this have been the cult of the Aga, or some equivalent archaic form of heavy iron stove, and the introduction of a range of bright colours as an alternative to white or cream.

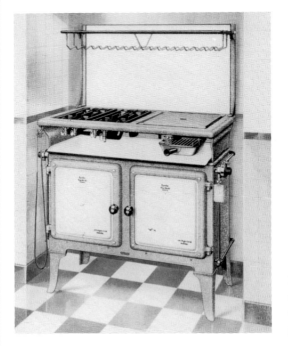

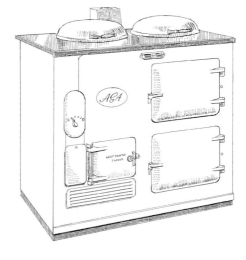

Left: *A 1930s gas double-oven, with a large boiling and grilling hotplate, and plate rack.*

Above: *A 1939 model of an Aga, which included a back boiler that provided hot water for the house.*

FIREPLACE
PRACTICALITIES

Choosing a Period Fireplace

Over the last decade or so it has become increasingly fashionable to restore original period fireplaces to full working order, or re-install them where they have previously been either removed and the hearth bricked-up, or replaced with a modern gas or electric fire. The reasons for doing this are often both aesthetic and symbolic. On the one hand the re-installation of a period fireplace restores the architectural and decorative focus and balance of a room to that which was originally intended when the house was built. On the other hand a fire that produces real flames appeals to a primitive instinct and creates a sense of coziness and well-being rarely provided by central heating and many modern gas and electric fires.

Ironically, the fashion for restoring fireplaces in an authentic period setting has undoubtedly been fuelled by advances in technology. More specifically, the considerable improvements made to flame-effect coal and log gas fires – to the point where they can be indistinguishable from the real thing – has meant that home-owners can enjoy the heat and appearance of a traditional fire without having to endure the labour-intensive business of making-up a new fire and clearing away the ashes every day. (Although burning coal and logs, where fuel regulations allow it, is of course an option that many still prefer.)

Similarly, the ever-increasing availability of authentic period fireplaces and fire-surrounds from specialist suppliers has made restoration a much easier option for home-owners than it has been in the past. A wide range of original fireplaces are available from specialist shops and architectural salvage companies (names and addresses are listed in the Directory, see pages 122–4). Alternatively, high-quality reproduction fireplaces which are often indiscernible from the originals, produced in marble, stone, cast-iron, wood, slate and plaster, are also widely available

Above: *The combination of a black marble surround, pale marble slips and a gilt overmantel mirror, set against a golden-yellow background, are used to create a Regency style interior.*

Left: *A New York apartment decorated in an 18th-century French style – the focal point of which is an imported 18th-century, Louis-style, marble chimneypiece.*

in every conceivable style, as is an enormous range of reproduction fireplace impedimenta, including tiles, andirons, dog grates, fenders, fire screens, pokers, brushes, tongs and scuttles. (Again, the names and addresses of suppliers are listed in the Directory.)

If you have decided to install a period fireplace probably the main difficulty nowadays lies in choosing the "right" model for the date of the house or the style of the room: a wrong choice, or mismatch will look badly out of place. In this context the illustrations and descriptions in Fireplace Styles (see pages 18–77) should be used as reference for choosing a correct style for a particular period. It is important to remember, however, that in previous centuries, particularly the 19th and early 20th, the designs of earlier periods were often revived and became fashionable once again. For example, in addition to contemporary designs, it was quite common to find copies of Queen Anne and Adamesque Georgian style fireplaces in the drawing rooms of Edwardian townhouses.

Scale is, of course, just as important as style: larger, and more elaborate fireplaces were invariably installed in large or more important rooms, such as the main reception rooms and master bedrooms; smaller, and generally plainer, surrounds were intended for smaller and less important rooms. The size of fireplace will of course be largely determined by the dimensions of the chimney breast and the hearth, together with the height of the ceiling. Before buying an original or reproduction fireplace it is important to take measurements – an overly large or unduly small fireplace will almost certainly look out of place.

Over the following pages you will find practical information on how to install a working period fireplace, including guidelines on what you can do yourself and when you should or must employ professional help. Among the topics discussed are: repairing and sweeping flues and hearths, fuel regulations and laying a traditional fire, laying on a gas supply, repairing and decorating fire-surrounds, restoring grates and ceramic tiles, making a decoupage fire screen, and decorating the mantel shelf and hearth with period ornaments and other paraphernalia associated with the fireplace.

Left: *Tripartite decoration of the walls and a gray marble fireplace with neo-Classical detailing contribute to the late-Victorian feel of this interior.*

Above: *This modern interpretation of a 19th-century interior includes a marbled wooden fire-surround and High Victorian "clutter" on the mantel shelf.*

A Working Fireplace

More historic houses are destroyed by fires caused by defective chimneys or hearths than from virtually any other cause. Similarly, blocked or damaged flues can impede the escape of smoke and gases such as carbon monoxide, with potentially lethal consequences for the occupants of the house. Consequently, it is vital that these are all checked and, if necessary, restored to good condition when re-installing a working period fireplace. In many countries it is illegal for this work to be carried out by anybody other than a professionally qualified and/or licensed individual or company. The same applies to laying on a gas supply for flame effect coal or log gas fires. Even where such restrictions do not exist it is strongly recommended, for your own safety, that you do not attempt any repairs and restorations stipulated, over the following pages, as unsuitable DIY projects.

CHIMNEYS

The efficient operation of an open fire is dependent upon two main factors: air for combustion must be drawn from the room into the grate, and the hot smoke and gases produced by the combustion process must rise up the flue and out of the top of the chimney, rather than back into the room. To facilitate this most chimneys, particularly those from the 19th and 20th centuries, are constructed along the following lines.

Firstly, the sides of the hearth opening are often splayed to maximize the flow of combustion air from the room to the grate. If any of the fire-

Below: *For fires to work efficiently and safely they need a constant supply of fresh air. Traditionally, draughts from cracks* *under doors and around windows were sufficient, but today's double-glazed rooms should be ventilated with airbricks.*

bricks are cracked they should be replaced or repaired with fireproof cement. While repairing firebricks with cement is a suitable project for DIY enthusiasts, replacing firebricks ideally should be carried out by a qualified builder or a company specialising in the installation and renovation of fireplaces.

Secondly, in most 19th- and 20th-century fireplaces the opening above the fire into the chimney flue is constructed from corbelled brickwork to form an inverted funnel (with a curved profile) that guides the ascending hot smoke and gases into the bottom of the flue. If they are damaged, the corbelled bricks must be replaced or repaired – a skilled job which should be left to a qualified bricklayer.

Thirdly, the flue, which takes a gently curving route up to the chimney stack (see the diagram on the right) must be free from any blockages. In older houses there have been instances of a section of a flue collapsing internally. Although this is rare, it should be checked out by a specialist fireplace company, who can carry out a simple test. (Note that in the unlikely event of a collapse, any repairs will be expensive.)

The chimney flue must also be swept clean. Even flues which have not served a solid fuel fire for years and have an intact smooth lining (either of cow-dung pargeting or cement-mortar and ox hair) will contain large deposits of soot. If these are not removed a chimney fire may well result once a new fire is lit. Nowadays, chimney sweeps use vacuum cleaners which produce none of the mess associated with traditional methods of brush cleaning.

Fourthly, for hot smoke and gases to escape from the chimney pots they must be shielded from down-draughts, which are a particular problem with chimneys sited below the ridge of

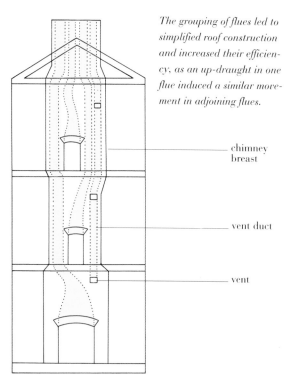

The grouping of flues led to simplified roof construction and increased their efficiency, as an up-draught in one flue induced a similar movement in adjoining flues.

chimney breast

vent duct

vent

the main roof on the leeside of the house, or those crowning the apex of lower roofs on the leeside of the main roof. The traditional remedy for down-draughts naturally occurring in these positions is either a metal pipe extension with a conical cowl fitted to the top of the pot, or a circular deflector (see the diagram, below left). It is not unusual for these to be missing or damaged especially in cases where open fires have not been used for some time. Together with any missing or damaged chimney pots, these must be either replaced or repaired by a qualified builder before a new fire is lit. Failure to do this will almost certainly result in clouds of smoke entering the room in question.

HEARTHS

In addition to making any necessary repairs to the sides of the hearth, it is very important to ensure that the bed of the hearth is incombustible and in good condition. Major repairs to brickwork are best carried out by a qualified builder. However, removal of old hearths, minor repairs and tiling are suitable DIY projects (see Installing an Edwardian Fireplace, page 86, and Repairing Tiles, page 108).

One thing to watch out for on any floors above ground level is a missing concrete infill (usually tiled on top and supported on a trimmer

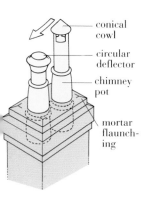

conical cowl

circular deflector

chimney pot

mortar flaunching

Two 19th-century chimney pots. The one on the right has been extended with a conical cowl; the one on the left with a circular deflector. Both are intended to inhibit down-draughts (which result in smoke being blown back into the room). The circular deflector can be more efficient at allowing the escape of hot gases from the fire.

arch built of splayed wooden blocks (see the diagram on the right). The inclusion of a concrete infill, typical in Victorian houses, but sometimes removed during subsequent "improvements", is vital if you are to avoid setting fire to floor joists, floorboards, or the ceiling below. A qualified builder or fireplace installation company should be consulted to ascertain if replacement or repairs are necessary.

GRATES

Cast-iron register grates (either combined with the fire-surround or fixed independently into the chimneypiece), dog grates (basket grates) and andirons may well need repairing. Having been subjected to heat over the years, grates may have become distorted and, in some instances, may be cracked. Repairs should be carried out by a specialist fireplace company, or a blacksmith with suitable experience. If the damage is particularly bad, replacement (either original or reproduction) may be a preferable solution.

It is quite common to find that cast-iron grates and surrounds have been painted at some point,

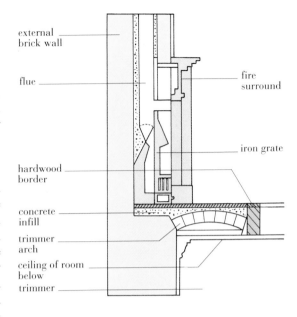

external brick wall

flue

fire surround

iron grate

hardwood border

concrete infill

trimmer arch

ceiling of room below trimmer

Above: *When re-installing a fireplace in an upstairs room, make sure the* incombustible trimmer arch and concrete infill have not been removed.

Left: *Most cast-iron register grates incorporate a damper below the front bars, which can be opened or closed to regulate the amount of air drawn into the fire. In an open position the fire will burn more fiercely, because of the greater amount of oxygen present. In a closed position, less oxygen results in slower combustion which is necessary if the fire is to be kept going overnight.*

often obscuring the decorative elements. To reveal these elements the paint should be removed and the cast-iron black-leaded (see Stripping a Cast-iron Fireplace, pages 106–7).

TRADITIONAL FUELS

Global concerns about air-pollution have meant that in most countries, and particularly in towns and cities, there are legally enforceable restrictions on the types of fuel that can be burnt in an open fire or stove. You must check with your local authority and/or the department of the environment to ascertain what is and is not allowed in your area. Smokeless fuel is available from coal merchants.

Where logs can be burnt, mainly in rural areas, it is important that the logs have been allowed to dry out thoroughly so as to avoid difficulties in lighting, keeping the fire alight and avoiding filling the room with smoke. (Coals should also be kept in a dry storage area, such as a cellar or coal-hole, before use.) It is also worth consulting local log suppliers about the different types of logs available in your area. For example, many fruit woods, such as apple, emit a very pleasant sweet smell when lit. Pine also has a distinctive fragrance.

FLAME-EFFECT COAL AND LOG GAS FIRES

With the advent of fuel restrictions, coal and log gas fires have increased in popularity over the last two or three decades. Today the range of authentic-looking coal and log gas fires is extensive. Styles to suit all manner of fireplaces from different periods are available.

The installation of a gas supply and a burner unit, which can be manufactured to the appropriate size (see Installing an Edwardian Fireplace, pages 86–9), should be carried out by either a qualified gas-fitter or a specialist fireplace company. A faulty installation can be very dangerous, and could lead to either an explosion, a fire or a build-up of toxic fumes, such as carbon monoxide.

Also, given the gradual wear and tear on components over the years, if you have acquired an early gas coal or log fire it should be checked and serviced by a qualified fitter before re-use.

Laying a coal or log fire

1 Fill the base of the grate with two or three layers of paper balls. These are made by scrunching up individual sheets of old newspaper into ball shapes. If you have a dog grate lay the paper balls between the andirons on either side of the hearth.
2 Place some kindling (dry and finely cut small pieces and splinters of wood) or fragments of wax and paraffin fire lighters at random on top of the paper balls.
3 Pile one or two layers of coal or slightly larger pieces of wood on top of the paper balls.
4 If there is one, slide open the damper grill (often fitted at the front of the grate) to maximize the intake of air from the room. Once the fire has got going it is usually best to close the damper so as to regulate the amount of heat escaping up the chimney.
5 Light the paper balls in three or four randomly spaced places or if there is one fitted, ignite a gas poker and insert it between the paper balls and the coals.
6 To assist the burning paper in heating up and igniting the coals or logs, you can use fire bellows (which increase the amount of oxygen required for the combustion process).
7 Once the fire is alight, gradually add more layers of coal or larger logs, taking care not to apply too much early on, or you will dampen down the fire and possibly extinguish it.

Installing an Edwardian Fireplace

MATERIALS AND EQUIPMENT:
- Crow bar
- Bolster and hammer
- Spirit level
- Straight edge
- Pencil
- Builder's trowel
- Plasterer's float
- Plasterer's hawk
- Spade
- Metal saw and file
- Containers for mixing mortar and plaster
- Building bricks
- Concrete lintel
- Strips of brickwork angle bead
- Bonding plaster
- Finish plaster
- Soft sand, lime, cement – ratios for mix are 4:1:1 respectively
- Builder's rubble
- 4 brass mirror clips
- 4 7.5cm/3in no.12 screws
- 4 rawlplugs
- Screwdriver
- Power drill and extension cable
- Ceramic floor tiles
- Tile cutter and tile file
- Flooring grade tile adhesive
- Powdered or pre-mixed tile grout (caulk)
- Clean, lint-free rag
- Lubricant, such as WD40

This project involved removing a modern York stone fireplace that had been installed in the dining room of an Edwardian house during the early 1970s, and replacing it with an original fireplace from one of the bedrooms in the same house. While many stages of the installation process are suitable for someone experienced in DIY, for reasons of safety others (stipulated below) should be left to a qualified professional – indeed, in some countries this is a legal requirement.

A gas coal fire was fitted in the hearth. Because of the dangers of carbon monoxide, before proceeding you must ensure that the following Building Regulations are fulfilled. The flue must have a minimum diameter of 17.5cm/7in – although preferably 22.5cm/9in – and any throat restrictors or dampers must be completely removed. The hearth must be fixed, non-combustible, and at least 30cm/12in deep and 7.5cm/3in thick. The room must have a minimum ventilation of 100sq cm/15¼sq in from outside air. A smoke test should be conducted by a qualified professional before commencing installation, to ensure that the flue has no leaks or blockages, and any necessary repairs made (warning: repairing a flue can be very expensive). Finally, the chimney should be swept before the fire is lit.

You should note that the cast-iron insert of the Edwardian fireplace was restored (by shot blasting) off site. If you wish to carry out the restoration yourself by using paint stripper, you should refer to the relevant instructions and illustrations on pages 106–7. The wooden surround was sanded and repainted.

1

1 **The 1970s York stone fireplace in situ. Before removing an existing fireplace arrange for a** qualified professional to disconnect the gas supply, together with the gas fire itself (if there is one).

2 If you are replacing an existing fireplace, remove, in sequence, the existing tiled plinth, the mantel shelf and the brick surround. You will almost certainly need a crow bar and some help to do this. The brick surround will invariably be secured to the wall with screws and mirror clips. If the screws have seized up they will have to be prized out.

3 If necessary, make good the base of the hearth with a mortar mix consisting of sand, lime and cement in a ratio of 4:1:1. Allow the mortar to dry thoroughly. In this instance, to accommodate the dimensions of the York stone fireplace, the original opening of the fireplace had been reduced by the installation of brick pillars and a concrete lintel. If the new fireplace you are fitting is larger than the previous fireplace, as here, you should remove the brick pillars and lintel with a bolster and chisel.

4 To accommodate the new cast-iron insert, measure the height, width and depth. Then build up new brick pillars either side of the opening and place a concrete lintel across the top of the pillars. (The measurement of the opening should be smaller than the outside measurement of the insert.) Make sure that the sides of the insert will just overlap the inside edges of the bricks and that the top edge of the insert will just overlap the bottom edge of the lintel. Use a spirit level to ensure that the columns are true. Next fill in the space between the top of the lintel and the original brick arch above with bricks and mortar. (The mortar mix you should use for the bricklaying is: sand, lime and cement in a ratio of 6:1:1.) Again, allow the mortar to dry thoroughly.

2

3

4

5

6

7

8

5 Next the chimney breast has to be prepared to accommodate the fire surround. Position the surround flush against the chimney breast and centre over the opening of the hearth. Use a spirit level to check that the horizontal and vertical are true, wedging a sliver of wood or cardboard under the bottom of the jambs if necessary. Then mark the wall around the outside of the surround with a pencil, adding an extra 5cm/2in all round.

6 Remove the surround and, using a bolster and chisel, cut out all the plaster inside the pencil lines to expose the brickwork. Next tile and grout (caulk) the base of the hearth. You must use floor-

ing-grade tiles. Note that you do not need to tile right to the back of the hearth – only as far as the back of the cast-iron insert so that the insert sits on the tiles.

Once the tiles have been laid you should remove the sections of skirting (base) board on either side of the chimney breast and arrange for the gas pipe to be installed from the gas tap (a brass upright restric-tor elbow with a removable nursery cock) at the side of the fire along the base of the brickwork (cutting out a small notch to accommodate the pipe if neces-sary) and around one side of the hearth. The pipe should then be run across to the centre back of the hearth and turned at 90 degrees to face forward so that it can travel through the centre of the base of the cast-iron insert.

7 Stand the cast-iron insert in position against the opening to the hearth (temporarily supporting it with a spade or shovel). Then re-position the fire-surround against the centre of the chimney breast, and adjust the position of the insert so that the edges of the jambs and frieze of the surround overlap it.

8 Note the position of the gas pipe in relation to the base of the insert. You may have to cut or file a small notch in the base (as here) to accommodate the pipe.

9 Remove the fire surround and fill in the gap between the wall and the insert with the same mortar mixture you used to repair the base of the hearth. Depending on the size of the gap, you may need to insert strips of brickwork angle bead between the sides of the insert and the bricks in order to hold the mortar mix in position (although this was not necessary in this case). You should also protect the tiles below with an old sheet or blanket.

10 To secure the surround to the chimney breast, screw four mirror clips (two each side) to the back of the surround. They should be positioned approximately 15cm/6in from the top and bottom of the surround. Place the surround against the chimney breast and mark the wall where the mirror clips fall. Remove the surround, drill four holes in the chimney breast and insert rawlplugs. Reposition the surround against the chimney breast and screw to the wall.

Next, dampen the surrounding brickwork with water and, using a float and trowel, make good the plasterwork around the surround with bonding. (Note, bonding plaster dries quicker than browning plaster and has a more adhesive quality.) Once the plaster has dried sufficiently (24-8 hours, depending on room temperature) apply a thin skim of finish plaster so that it is flush with the surround.

11 Back fill behind the cast-iron insert with brick rubble up to approximately 2.5cm/1in from the top of the insert. Next, level off the top of the rubble with a mixture of 4 parts soft sand to one part lime. Using a trowel and a mortar mix consisting of 6 parts sand: 1 part lime: 2 parts cement, seal the gap between the insert and the back of the chimney breast at an angle of 45 degrees, and allow to dry.

10

11

12

13

14

15

16

12 If you have a removable hood clip it into the slots at the top of the centre of the insert. (You may have a cast-iron rather than a copper hood, but they are attached in the same way.)

13 To ensure that there is adequate ventilation in the room, and a sufficient up-draught for the fire to work efficiently, you must install a ventilation grill either in an outside wall or, if there is a ventilated space below the floorboards, in the floor. (Refer to the introduction on page 86 for the dimensions of the grill.)

14 Place the burner unit in position. (The burner unit here was made especially to fit the hearth but you can buy complete kits containing burner unit,

embers and coals.) Arrange for a qualified gas fitter to connect the gas pipe to the burner unit, and to check connections for leaks.

15 Clip the bars into position on the front of the insert and place the ember material and coals on top of the silica bed of the burner unit (in accordance with the manufacturer's instructions). No particular arrangement is required as far as the coals are concerned, but do not pack them too tightly – a loose stack will allow air into the heart of the fire, giving a better flame and glow.

16 To finish attach new sections of skirting (base) board to the chimney breast on either side of the surround and decorate accordingly.

17 To prevent the cast-iron insert rusting apply a thin coat of a lubricant such as WD40 every 3 months; for the copper hood use a proprietary copper polish. The fire should be lit in accordance with the manufacturer's instructions. Always pull the hood to the open, rather than closed, position when the fire is lit, otherwise discolouration will soon occur. You will also achieve a better updraft with the hood in this position.

18 The wooden surround was painted white. Most fireplaces of this period and style were painted. (If you want a wooden finish see page 102.) To complement the fireplace an Edwardian cast-iron fender has been added and a selection of Edwardian vases contributes to the period feel.

Marble, Stone and Slate Fireplaces

Materials such as marble, stone and slate convey an air of solidity, formality and, in some cases, opulence, so it is not surprising that they have traditionally been used in the making of fireplaces, particularly those designed for the more prestigious rooms in the house. Like most natural materials, they are prone to wear and tear. Fortunately, cleaning and minor repairs are well within the scope of the home owner.

REPAIRING CRACKS AND CHIPS

Repairing very large cracks in marble, stone and slate is beyond the scope of the amateur, and should be left to a specialist fireplace company (see the Directory, pages 122–4). However, you can make good small chips and cracks in marble, stone and slate with a proprietary epoxy-resin glue and filler designed for the purpose (following the manufacturer's instructions). When dry, rub down with a fine grade wet-and-dry paper to the shape of the surrounding area. Blend in marble repairs using the techniques and paints and glazes shown for faux marble effects on the following pages.

A typical Greek-revival, white marble fireplace with subtle blue and gray primary and secondary veining. Imported Classical fireplaces such as this were installed in many New York houses during the 1830s.

REMOVING DIRT AND STAINS

Marble, stone and slate are prone to general discolouration and a variety of stains such as rust, mildew and coal dust. While a range of proprietary cleaners is now available, most traditional methods of cleaning remain just as effective.

Initially try to remove dirt and grime from marble by washing down with warm soapy water and rinsing. If any grime or stains remain, try adding half a cup of ammonia to a bucket of soapy water. If this fails you should apply a poultice (see below). Sandstone, limestone and slate should also be cleaned with a poultice, although you can usually remove soot stains from slate by simply gently scrubbing down with warm soapy water, and then rinsing. Fly marks can be removed from all surfaces by first moistening them with a little white spirit (mineral spirits), nudging them off with a blunt sliver of wood, and then gently rubbing over the area with a chamois leather. Algae or mildew, provided it is caught early, responds to a little ammonia mixed with soapy water. If it is extensive, apply a poultice.

APPLYING A POULTICE

This is one of the most effective methods of cleaning marble, scagliola, stone and slate. The constituents of the poultice vary. For light stains, mix up a thick paste with sepiolite powder and distilled water and apply either over the affected area or the entire surface in a 2cm/¾in thick layer. Leave for between four to eight hours and then brush and wipe off, and rinse thoroughly. For grease, oil or wax stains, or when treating slate, use white spirit (mineral spirits) instead of water to make the paste. For particularly stubborn stains add a little methylated spirits (denatured alcohol) to the white spirit, and when treating mildew add a little ammonia.

POLISHING AND FINISHING

To tone up the finish of marble you can rub in milk, or a hard, white polish, leave for about an hour and then buff with a soft rag. To revive slate, mix white spirit (mineral spirits) and boiled linseed oil in equal proportions, and apply sparingly with a wad of cotton wool wrapped inside a double layer of cotton rag, rubbing well

Above: *A stone fireplace, with traditional arched opening, stop-chamfered jambs and plain spandrels.*

The fireplace was cleaned when the rest of the house, built in the 1720s, was recently restored.

Left: *A Victorian slate chimney-piece, c. 1880, with a simulated marble finish that sets off the cast-iron register grate and floral tiled cheeks.*

Above: *An original and very plain marble fire-surround, with a matching raised marble hearth projecting*

into the main reception room of a small terraced cottage, built c.1840, in Chelsea, London.

into the surface. Treat friable stone by brushing on a solution of one part acrylic matte medium to every ten parts of distilled water.

FAUX MARBLE

The painting of wooden fire-surrounds in imitation of more prestigious and expensive marbles began on a large scale during the Renaissance in Italy and France, and became fashionable in Britain, North America and the rest of Europe from the 17th century onward following the adoption of the various classically-inspired styles of architecture and design. The impetus to fake

the real thing was fuelled by the considerable cost of quarrying, cutting, polishing and transporting marble.

The range of copied marbles was as extensive as the varieties of the original material – which even in the 17th century ran into hundreds. Faux marble is a pastiche of marble but, if executed sympathetically is no less effective for that. At its most sophisticated, as seen in the work of two of its greatest exponents, Thomas Kershaw and John Taylor, during the 19th century, it can be a replication of marble that maintains the illusion even under the closest scrutiny.

White and Gray Faux Marble

In all types of marble there are subtle depths and gradations of colour, together with a series of major and minor veins that lie on or close to the surface. To mimic these successfully you should not only carefully study the illustrations that accompany the following step-by-step instructions, but also, if at all possible, take a close look at the real thing. Examples of different types of marble can be found in many museums, as well as among the stock of specialist fireplace and architectural salvage companies. Practising the faux marbling technique on spare off-cuts of wood before you begin in earnest is also strongly recommended.

Mixing glazes

To produce the faux marble finishes here and on the following pages you will need to mix various oil-based glazes. These are made up of pigments (artist's oils) suspended in a clear medium and thinned with a solvent to make them semi-transparent when applied over an opaque groundcoat. The tinted semi-transparent glaze allows the underlying ground colour to "ghost" through it, thereby creating subtle combinations, depths and gradations of colour.

The recipe for each glaze gives the approximate proportions of each pigment in relation to any other pigments included, the approximate proportions of solvent in relation to the clear medium; and the approximate proportions of combined pigments in relation to the combined solvent and medium. For example, in glaze A for the white and gray faux marble the pigment consists of 3 parts raw umber artist's oil, to 3 parts black artist's oil, to 2 parts veridian artist's oil. The medium consists of 3 parts transparent oil glaze to 2 parts white spirit (mineral spirits). When mixed together the proportion (or ratio) of combined pigments to medium in the glaze equals 1 part pigment to 30 parts medium.

The actual quantity of glaze you require depends upon the absorbancy of the underlying surface and how thickly you apply the glaze. Consequently, it is virtually impossible to prescribe exact quantities. However, a useful rule of thumb is: 250ml/10fl.oz of glaze to cover a surface of approximately 7sq m/7½sq yd.

So, for example, to mix approximately 250ml/10fl oz of glaze A for the white and gray faux marble you should:

1 Using an old artist's fitch brush to blend thoroughly, mix 150ml/6fl.oz of transparent oil glaze with 100ml/4fl.oz of white spirit (mineral spirits) to make the medium. Mix in a 1 litre/¼ gal metal or plastic paint kettle.

2 Squeeze the artist's oils from their tubes into another container. The pigments (artist's oils) are mixed together in a ratio of 3 parts raw umber to 3 parts black to 2 parts veridian.

3 Pour a little of the blended clear medium into a third container and, again using an old artist's fitch, slowly blend in the pigments (artist's oils) from the second container. You will end up with a coloured liquid of cream-like consistency that should match the relevant colour swatch (right). Do not worry about the translucency of the glaze – just the colour match. Add more pigments if required.

4 Again, using an old artist's fitch, gradually stir the coloured, cream-like liquid into the bulk of the clear medium that remains in the first container. From time to time swatch a little of the colour over the white eggshell groundcoat to test the translucency of the glaze. Add more medium to increase the translucency and more pigment(s) to increase the opacity, but in each case make sure you thoroughly blend the mixture.

Note: The oil-based glaze described above is the type generally used by professional, specialist decorators. However, you can also mix an oil-based glaze by using flat-oil or eggshell paint, either pre-mixed or tinted to the desired colour with artist's oils, and thinned to the required degree of translucency by the addition of white spirit (mineral spirits).

MATERIALS & EQUIPMENT

- White wood primer
- White oil-based undercoat
- White oil-based eggshell
- Glazes: see below
- Clear satin or gloss polyurethane varnish
- 5cm/2in standard decorator's brush
- 2cm/¾in flat-bristled artist's brush
- 4cm/1½in standard decorator's brush
- 2.5cm/1in standard decorator's brush
- Large jamb duster brush
- Badger softener brush
- Clean lint-free rag

A
B
C
D

GLAZES

A *Artist's oils:* 3 parts raw umber, 3 parts black, 2 parts veridian. *Medium:* 3 parts transparent oil glaze, 2 parts white spirit (mineral spirits). Ratio: 1 part pigment, 30 parts medium.
B As glaze A above, but add ¼ part raw sienna artist's oil.
C As glaze A above, but add ¼ part more veridian and ¼ part more black artist's oils.
D *Artist's oils:* 2 parts raw umber, 2 parts black, 1 part veridian. *Medium:* 2 parts transparent oil glaze, 1 part white spirit (mineral spirits). Ratio: 1 part pigment, 7 parts medium.

Above: *A Victorian copy of a mid-18th-century white marble fireplace.*

1

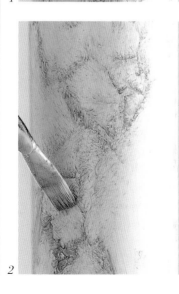

2

1 Having prepared, primed and undercoated the fire-surround, apply two base coats of white eggshell paint and allow 24 hours drying time after each one. Then, using a 5cm/2in standard decorator's brush, stipple on glaze A to form the basic shapes of the primary veins. To some extent the pattern you establish is a matter of personal composition, although you should refer to the illustration for guidance. Also note that the areas of the fire-surround where you apply the least glaze at this stage will later be the sites of the secondary veins. *Note:* It is advisable to marble one section of the fire-surround at a time. In other words, having applied the base coats to the entire surround, follow steps 1-8 on the left jamb first, the right jamb second, the frieze or lintel third and the mantel shelf fourth.

2 Use the bristle tips of a 2cm/¾in flat-bristled artist's brush to push and coalesce the glaze into the irregular-shaped links of the chain of primary veins.

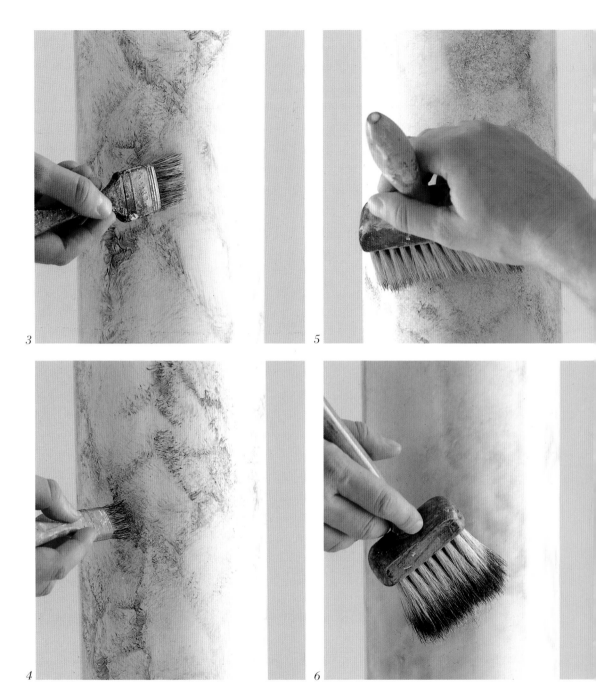

3 Employing the same technique as in 2 (on the previous
page), and using a 4cm/1½in
standard decorator's brush,
create the slightly fainter
secondary veins.

4 Dipping the bristles of a
4cm/1in standard decora-
tor's brush alternately into the
pale green and pale yellow

glazes, B and C, stipple on
translucent patches of broken
colour around the edges of the
primary veins.

5 Gently stipple over the still-
wet glazes with a large,
soft-bristled jamb duster brush
so as to get rid of any obtrusive
brush marks on the surface of
the fire-surround.

6 Lightly flick the bristle tips of
a badger softener over the wet
glazes to soften and blend the
primary and secondary veins.
Then allow the surface to dry for
24 hours.

7 Having wiped on a thin coat
of transparent oil glaze with
a clean rag, use a small, flat-
bristled artist's brush and glaze D

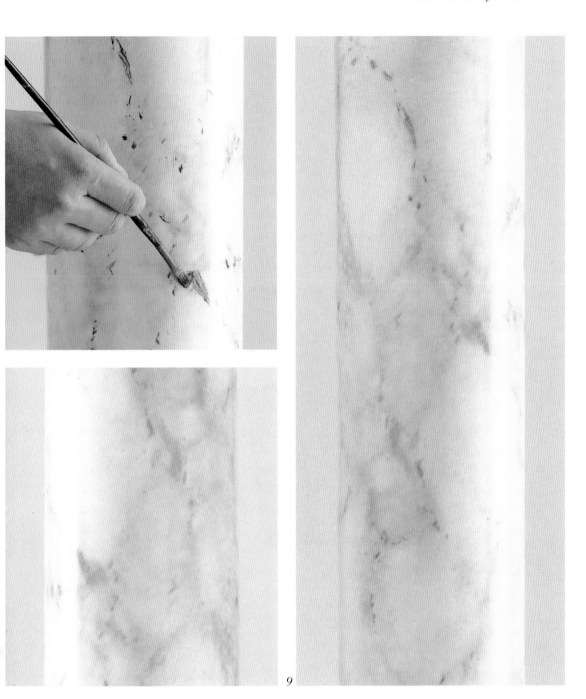

9

to create the irregular-shaped mineral deposits characteristic of the marble. *Note:* While most of the deposits lie along, or follow, the paths of the primary veins, there are a few isolated on the secondary veins.

8 Gently soften and blend the glazes with a badger softener immediately after you've brushed them on. Leave to dry for 24 hours. Then repeat steps 1-8 on the remaining sections of the fire-surround (refer to the *Note* in step 1 above for sequence).

9 Apply one or two coats of satin or gloss, clear polyurethane varnish to the entire surround, allowing 24 hours drying time between coats. Finally, for a more lustrous finish, polish with one or two applications of furniture wax.

Black and Gold Faux Marble

As with the white and gray faux marble on the preceding pages, you should, if at all possible, examine an actual example of black and gold marble in addition to following the illustrations shown here. By doing this you will learn a great deal about its subtle structure – notably the loosely linked, chain-like formation of veins that lie on or just below the surface. Also, as before, practise on some spare off-cuts of wood before you begin in earnest.

MATERIALS & EQUIPMENT
- White oil-based primer
- Gray oil-based undercoat
- Other paints and glazes: see below
- Satin or gloss clear polyurethane varnish
- Clean lint-free rag
- Transparent oil glaze
- 1.5cm/⅝in flat fitch brush
- Small badger softener brush
- Plastic eraser
- Small square-bristled artist's brush
- Cotton wool buds (swabs)
- 1.5cm/⅝in artist's brush
- Fine grade wet-and-dry paper

Left: *A mid-19th-century, Belgian black marble fireplace. It is very similar, in terms of colour and configuration of veins, to the illustrated black and gold faux marble.*

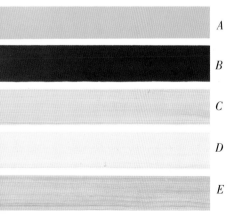

A

B

C

D

E

PAINTS AND GLAZES

For the method of mixing glazes, refer to page 94.

A Dark bamboo eggshell paint.
B Black eggshell paint.
C *Artist's oils:* 4 parts yellow ochre, 3 parts white, 2 parts burnt sienna. *Medium:* 2 parts transparent oil glaze, 1 part white spirit (mineral spirits). Ratio: 1 part pigment, 15 parts medium.

D *Artist's oils:* 10 parts white, 2 parts yellow ochre, 1 part burnt sienna. *Medium:* as in glaze C above. Ratios in glaze: 1 part pigment, 10 parts medium.
E *Artist's oils:* 1 part yellow ochre, 1 part burnt sienna, 1 part white. *Medium:* as in glaze C above. Ratios in glaze: 1 part pigment, 10 parts medium.

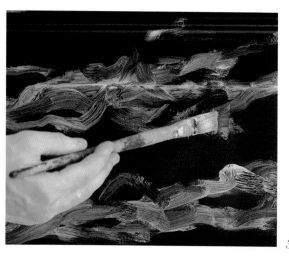

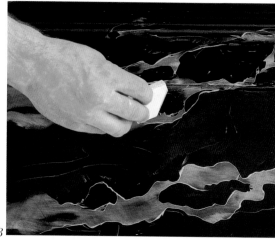

3

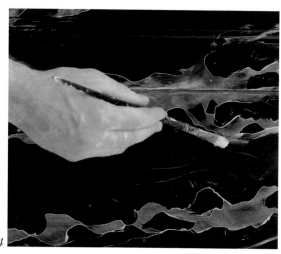

4

1 Apply two coats of black paint B to the previously prepared, primed and undercoated fire-surround. Leave to dry for 24 hours between coats.

Next, using a clean, lint-free rag, apply a thin coat of transparent oil glaze over the first section of the fire-surround. (*Note:* It is advisable to marble one section of the fire-surround at a time. In other words, having applied the base coats to the entire surround, follow steps 1–8 on the left jamb first, the right jamb second, the frieze or lintel third and the mantel shelf fourth.)

Then, using a 1.5cm/⅝in flat fitch brush, and dipping the bristles alternately into glazes

C, D and E, loosely brush on the basic shapes of the veining chains. As you can see in the illustration, the colours of each chain subtly change along their lengths – hence the use of three glazes.

2 Soften and blend each chain immediately after you've completed it, by lightly brushing the wet glazes with the bristle tips of a small badger softener.

3 Pull the hard edge of a plastic eraser through the wet glaze to cut out and reinforce the basic shape of the veins. Although this looks complicated, by copying the illustration and practising the technique on an off-cut of wood you will soon learn how to move

the glaze over the surface, coalescing it into thin, hard edges, and thus defining the irregular-shaped links that make up the major chains. *Note:* As you work, keep wiping off the build-up of glaze on the eraser onto a rag.

4 Using a small, square-bristled artist's brush, and again dipping into glazes C, D and E, apply the thin filaments that either shoot out of, or in some cases link, sections of the main veining chains. As you can see, the shape of these filaments varies. However, you will find that they all broadly follow the predominantly diagonal accent of the main veins.

5 Repeat the technique with the hard-edged eraser shown in step 3 (on previous page) to extend and further define the shape of the thin filaments introduced in the last step.

6 Use the tip of a cotton swab to carefully remove any spots of glaze left in and between the main veins.

7 Lightly soften and blend the filaments and veins using a badger softener brush, as in step 2. Allow to dry for 24 hours.

8 Mix a pale white glaze from 1 part white artist's oil to 10 parts of a medium made up of equal quantities of transparent oil glaze and white spirit (mineral spirits).

Then, wipe a thin coat of transparent oil glaze over the surface with a clean, lint-free rag, then apply the white glaze with a small artist's brush to form the secondary (ghost) veins that link the major veins and filaments. Soften and blend each vein with a badger softener immediately after brushing it on.

9 Mix up another translucent white glaze, this time consisting of 1 part white artist's oil to

5

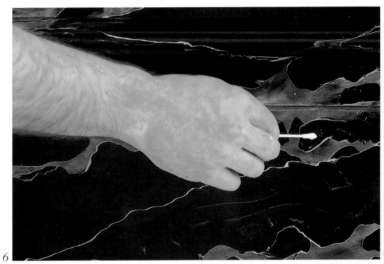

6

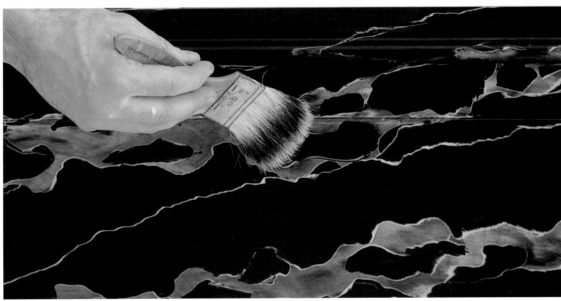

7

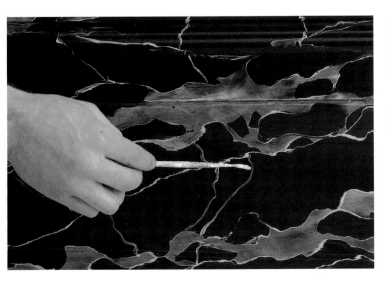

approximately 35 parts of a medium again consisting of equal quantities of transparent oil glaze and white spirit (mineral spirits).

Then, using a 1.5cm/¾in artist's brush, apply the glaze to form the oval-shaped fossil forms that lie just below the surface and in and between the main veining chains. Again, soften and blend each group of fossil forms with a badger softener brush immediately after you have brushed them on.

10 Allow the surface to dry thoroughly for approximately 24 hours. Then repeat steps 1-9 on the remaining sections of the fire-surround (refer to the *Note* in step 1 for recommended sequence).

11 Finally, when you have marbled all the sections, you should apply one or two coats of satin or gloss, clear polyurethane varnish, allowing 24 hours drying time between coats. For a more lustrous finish, the surface can be gently rubbed down with fine-grade, wet-and-dry paper prior to polishing with one or two applications of furniture wax.

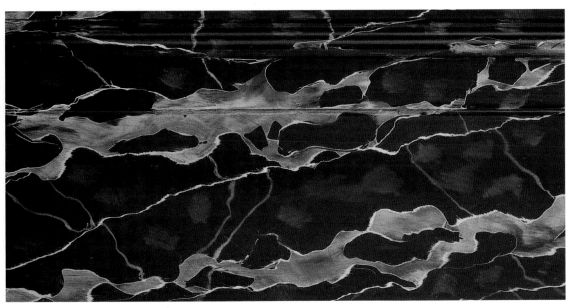

Restoring a Wooden Fire-Surround

In addition to paints and glazes, stains and varnishes have been traditionally used to produce a decorative finish on wooden fire-surrounds. While paints provide an opaque coloured finish that covers the underlying wood, and when combined with translucent glazes simulate other materials, such as marble (see pages 94–101), stains and varnishes either change or enhance the natural colour of the wood without concealing its figuring or graining. Consequently, it is almost always hardwoods, which, unlike most softwoods, display an infinite variety of attractive figuring and graining, that are finished in this manner. Stained and varnished mahogany and oak have been the most commonly used hardwoods for fire-surrounds. However, some softwoods, such as pine, can also be successfully stained and varnished, as illustrated here.

An alternative to stripping off paint and varnish using the method described below is to employ a commercial stripping company, who will remove the surround, dip it in a tank of caustic soda (lye), apply coats of acetic acid to neutralize the caustic, and then allow the surround to dry thoroughly before re-installing it.

The Edwardian pine fire-surround below had been painted and a gas fire installed. It was restored by stripping off the paint, mahogany staining the wood and installing a gas coal fire (see the finished fireplace opposite).

Preparation

Before staining and varnishing a wooden fire-surround you will have to remove any layers of paint that have been applied since it was installed. Proceed as follows:

1 Open windows and doors to ensure adequate ventilation.

2 Put on goggles, a face mask and chemical-resistant household gloves to protect eyes, lungs and hands.

3 Brush on several coats of spirit-based paint stripper.

4 Leave the stripper on until the paint begins to bubble and blister, then scrape off the paint with a metal scraper and medium grade wire (steel) wool. Always work in the direction of the grain of the wood, and use a small brush to remove paint debris from the recesses of any mouldings.

Note: Motifs and decorations on some old wooden fire-surrounds are made from gesso – a plaster-like material – and are glued on to the surface. Take great care not to damage these applied mouldings as they can be quite delicate. If damage does occur, or pieces are missing, repairs can be made by applying a pre-mixed synthetic gesso (available from specialist decorating suppliers). This synthetic gesso can be applied straight from the can and

then moulded and sanded to the right shape.

5 You will almost certainly need to brush on additional coats of stripper, as all the layers of paint are unlikely to come off in one go.

6 When all the paint has been removed, rub down the exposed wood with a rag soaked in white spirit (mineral spirits) in order to neutralize any residue of stripper left on the surface of the surround. Then allow to dry thoroughly.

Note: Old coats of varnish should be removed using a commercial varnish stripper and the method described above.

Finishing

To prepare the bare wood for staining and varnishing:

1 Cover any exposed nail or screw heads with two coats of metal primer.

2 Fill any holes or cracks in the wood with a commercial flexible wood filler. (These are available in a wide range of colours to match different woods.)

3 Once the filler has dried thoroughly rub it down with medium and then fine sandpaper, so that the repair is flush with the contours of the surrounding surface.

4 With woods such as pine cover any exposed knots with two or three coats of a commercial knotting compound, allowing each coat to dry thoroughly before applying the next one.

5 To stain the fire-surround you should use a commercial oil-based wood stain. These are available in a wide range of colours, such as brown and red mahogany, light and dark oak, and pale and antique pine. (It is best not to use water-based stains, as they tend to raise the grain of the wood, which then requires lightly sanding-down between coats.) The number of coats you apply depends on how dark you want the finish to be, but usually a minimum of two coats will be required. Drying times vary from about 24 to 36 hours. Once the stain has dried you should protect the finish by applying one or two coats of clear gloss, satin or matte polyurethane varnish.

Note: As an alternative to applying separate coats of stain and varnish, you can use a commercial coloured varnish which, like oil-based wood stains, is available in a range of natural wood colours.

Ageing Pine

During the past two decades it has become fashionable to strip the paint from pine fire-surrounds, and simply varnish or polish the bare wood. In so doing, carvings and mouldings which may have become partially obscured under accumulated layers of paint are restored to their original condition.

Virtually all fire-surrounds made of softwoods, such as pine, were originally intended to be painted; most hardwoods, such as mahogany, were stained and varnished or polished. However, what is considered aesthetically pleasing varies at different points in time. Just as the Victorians revived and adapted designs from previous centuries, so we at the end of the 20th century are changing styles and finishes to suit our own aesthetic. In that sense, staining or antiquing a pine fire-surround is not only decoratively legitimate, but will also become a period style in its own right.

The technique shown here for artificially ageing new or stripped pine can also be used to antique other pale woods, such as sycamore or birch. For darker woods, like mahogany or walnut, you would need to increase the proportions of powder pigment in the antiquing glaze to achieve the desired effect.

TO MAKE THE GLAZE:
- Mix 1 part raw sienna artist's powder pigment with 1 part raw umber artist's powder pigment, adding a little water until you have a coloured liquid with a creamy consistency.
- In a separate container mix a medium consisting of approximately 15 times the volume of the coloured liquid (above), and made up of 7 parts water to 3 parts PVA (white glue).
- Gradually add the medium to the coloured liquid to make the glaze, blending thoroughly. Test the glaze for strength of colour on an offcut of pine. Add a little more pigment if you wish to darken it.

Above: *An early Georgian, wooden pine surround, with simple incised mouldings and patterns on the lintel and jambs. Surrounds of this style were in common use from the 1720s onward. The majority of softwood surrounds were actually intended to be painted, in simulation of marble.*

1 Remove the layers of paint from the surface of the fire-surround following the method described on page 102. When using chemical paint strippers it is particularly important to ensure adequate ventilation in the room, wear plastic goggles to protect your eyes, a mask to prevent the inhalation of fumes, and household gloves to protect your hands and arms. Once any remnants of the chemical have been neutralized (again following the manufacturers instructions) and the fireplace has thoroughly dried, seal any knots in the wood with a minimum of two coats of a clear knotting compound (or clear shellac).

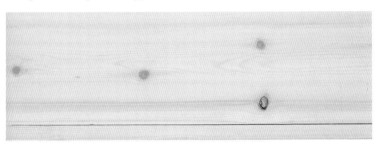

2 If the fire-surround is new pine you may wish to simulate some natural wear and tear. For example, evidence of woodworm infestation can be faked by making clusters of small holes with a nail or the point of a compass. Other signs of ageing, such as surface dents or small chips along the leading edges, can be made with careful use of a hammer or craft knife.

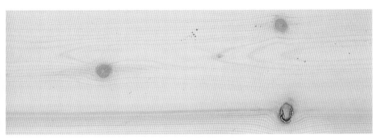

3 Using a standard decorator's brush, roughly brush on a liberal quantity of antiquing glaze over one section – such as the left jamb – of the fire-surround.

4 Make a flat pad of a clean, lint-free cotton rag and rub the glaze into the grain and the small holes and scratches in the wood, at the same time removing excess glaze from the surface. Keep turning the rag to form a clean pad as it becomes saturated with the glaze. Depending on the room temperature you have approximately one hour to complete this stage before the glaze dries. Then repeat steps 3–4 on the other sections of the fireplace – i.e., right jamb, lintel and mantel shelf in sequence.

5 Once the glaze has dried on all sections, step back, assess the finish and, if you wish to make it darker, repeat steps 3–4. Finally, to protect the finish, apply one or two coats of matte, satin or gloss clear polyurethane varnish (or matte, satin or gloss clear cellulose sealer).

Stripping and Restoring Cast Iron

To remove layers of paint from cast-iron fittings you can have them shot-blasted by a specialist fireplace company. This involves removing the fitting, renovating it in a workshop and re-installing it once the work has been completed (see Installing an Edwardian fireplace, pages 86–91). However, if you do not wish to have the fitting removed, it is well within the scope of the competent amateur to strip off the layers of paint in situ.

MATERIALS & EQUIPMENT
- Household gloves
- Plastic goggles
- Paint stripper – gel, paste, or powder mix – not liquid
- Metal or plastic scraper
- Plastic spatula
- Wire brush
- Metal filler (e.g. Plastic Padding)
- Rust remover
- Black grate polish
- Fire cement
- Old rags
- Soft duster
- Low-tack masking (drafting) tape

1

2

1 Remove any carpets, place old newspapers on the floor, mask off surrounding areas and open window and doors to ensure adequate ventilation. Wear goggles and household gloves to protect eyes and hands.

Use an old paintbrush to apply a liberal quantity of paint stripper over the surface of the cast iron, making sure you work it into the crevices. You should use a gel, paste or powder-mix stripper, in accordance with the manufacturer's instructions, rather than a liquid version. The latter will run off vertical surfaces and on to the floor.

2 Having left the stripper to react with the underlying paint for approximately two hours (it will bubble up in places), start to remove the residue with a metal or a plastic scraper.

3 Use a wire brush to remove the residue from the relief mouldings, working carefully on a section at a time, and making sure you don't splash yourself. A little hot water can be used to help remove particularly stubborn areas, but you may also need to make a further application of stripper, leaving it to react with the paint as before. Finish off by rubbing down with old rags.

4 Repair any small chips and cracks in the cast iron with a metal filler, such as Plastic Padding (available from auto

accessory shops). Mix the filler according to the manufacturer's instructions and press it into the damaged areas with a plastic spatula. You should shape the filler to the contours of the surrounding area before it has set. Once it has dried it is quite difficult to sand into shape.

Note: Repairing large cracks is beyond the scope of an amateur, and should be left a specialist fireplace or architectural salvage company. (This can be expensive, and will probably involve removing and re-installing the fitting. For advice on replacing missing parts, see Installing an Edwardian Fireplace, pages 86–91).

5 The sides and back of a cast-iron grate, those closest to the fire itself, will almost certainly be pitted with rust. Using a wire brush remove any loose rust on the surface and apply one or two coats of rust remover with an old paintbrush. The chemical reaction that takes places will convert the rust into an inert crust, which can be blacked or painted.

6 If the firebrick is made of brick, it may well be cracked. To repair this, remove any loose particles with a brush, mix up some fire cement according to the manufacturer's instructions, and work the cement into the cracks with a metal scraper. Smooth the repair flush with the surrounding area before the cement has had time to dry.

7 Once all surfaces have been allowed to dry thoroughly, black and polish the grate with a graphite paste (such as Zebrite which is available from hardware stores and specialist fireplace companies). Use a clean rag to rub a thin coat of the polish over the surface of the cast iron (and an old brush to get into the mouldings). Do not make the application too thick as this will be difficult to polish afterward.

8 Use a soft cloth to buff the surface of the cast iron. By leaving the recesses of the mouldings unpolished you will produce a pleasing contrast between the matte finish in the recessed areas and the soft sheen on the raised sections. The blacking will last up to six months, depending on how often you use the fire.

Repairing Tiles

MATERIALS & EQUIPMENT
- Scouring pad
- Metal scraper
- Paint stripper
- Old paintbrush
- White spirit (mineral spirits)
- Plaster filler, e.g. Polyfilla or Tetrion (spackle)
- PVA (white glue)
- Sandpaper
- Paper masking (drafting) tape
- Small artist's brushes
- Acrylic paints
- Clear glaze

Tiles were often used in Victorian cast iron fireplaces and if possible they should be retained, even if they have been damaged. New tiles can detract from the period feel.

The glazed clay tiles incorporated in the cheeks of this cast-iron fireplace are fixed to the ironwork from the back with a single bracket on either side. Because these brackets cannot be reached without removing the fireplace from the wall minor repairs to the tiles, or replacing single tiles, have to be carried out in situ.

1

1 Remove any layers of paint that may have been applied on top of the tiles by brushing on an application of commercial gel or paste paint stripper (do not use a liquid stripper as it will run off the vertical surfaces). Having left the stripper to react with the paint (the latter will begin to bubble up), scrub away the residue with a nylon scouring pad. Use a metal scraper to remove paint from the edges of the tiles. It is very important to work carefully throughout – you don't want to damage the glazed surface of the tiles. If the tiles are simply ingrained with dirt, clean with warm water and a non-abrasive detergent.

2 To repair a cracked or chipped tile, begin by cleaning the crack and surrounding area with a cloth and white spirit (mineral spirits). Next, tape the tile, as in the illustration, and fill the crack with some plaster filler (spackle) mixed with a little PVA (white glue). Once the filler has dried it can be gently sanded flush with the surrounding area.

If a tile is damaged beyond repair, it will have to be replaced.

3

Put on plastic goggles to protect your eyes, and gloves to protect your hands, and chip out the old tile with a hammer and cold chisel. Measure the height and width of the metal recess before purchasing either an original replacement or a reproduction tile (available from specialist suppliers, see the Directory, pages 122–4). The height of the replacement tile should be exactly the same as the height of the opening; its width should be slightly greater than the width of the opening. You should be able to buy a tile of the right size, but if not, buy a slightly larger tile that can be trimmed to size with a tile cutter or tile file. When the fit is right, apply fire cement to the back of the tile and the metal grooves of the opening. Carefully push the tile into position, using slivers of match sticks to hold the tile in place until the cement has dried.

4

3 To match the plaster(spackle) repair to the pattern of the surrounding tile, mix appropriately coloured acrylic paints with white acrylic paint on the back of a ceramic tile until you achieve the desired colour match. Then apply the paint sparingly with a small artist's brush, taking care not to brush paint on to the surrounding glaze. Allow to dry, then apply a coat of clear glaze (available from artists' suppliers) over the surface of the tile.

Découpage Fire Screen

MATERIALS AND EQUIPMENT
- Oil-based wood primer
- Mid-gray or pale green, oil-based undercoat
- Mid-dark green, matte-finish, oil-based top coat
- 5cm/2in standard decorator's brush
- Clear, satin-finish, acrylic varnish
- Gilt wax or cream
- Clean, lint-free rag
- Selection of reproduction Victorian, découpage paper cut-outs
- Short-bladed scissors
- Cow-gum or spray mount adhesive
- Mid-dark brown French polish (shellac)
- 5cm/2in varnishing brush

Also known as *art pauvre*, or poor man's art, découpage was a popular pastime, particularly among women and young ladies, during the second half of the 19th century. An inexpensive technique for decorating domestic items such as wooden boxes, free-standing folding partitions and fire screens, it involves cutting out paper scraps and pasting them on to the surface of an object. The images and motifs that were used varied enormously, but people (especially busts), animals, flowers and plants, were among the most common. The art of the technique, which if done well can be quite time-consuming, lies in the manner in which the images and motifs are positioned in relation to one another: the aim being to produce a carefully crafted and balanced composition.

Initially, practitioners of the art cut out their scraps from any available source, such as early magazines, Christmas cards and picture books. However, as the hobby became popular manufacturers began to print collections or books of scraps specifically designed for the purpose. Over the last decade or so, there has been a revival of interest in découpage, and various companies have started reproducing Victorian scraps (for names and addresses, see the Directory, pages 122–4). Similarly, a number of companies also offer ready-made, plain wooden fire screens (such as the fire screen illustrated below and opposite) intended for découpage decoration.

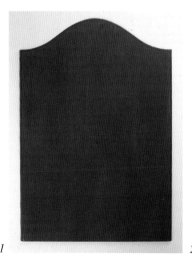

1

2

3

1 The wooden fire screen used for this project was bought ready-made. However, you could cut out your own from a sheet of MDF (medium density fibreboard), using the illustrations for guidance. Prime and undercoat the screen (and the two detach-able feet), and allow to dry. Next apply two coats of mid-dark green, matte-finish, oil-based paint, allowing 24 hours drying time between coats. Then apply one or two coats of clear, satin finish, acrylic varnish and, again, allow to dry thoroughly.

2 Using the tip of your finger, wipe a thin coat of gilt cream or wax around the perimeter moulding of the screen and the leading edges of the detachable feet. Once this has dried (approx. one hour), gently burnish with a small piece of clean, lint-free rag.

5

6

3 Lay the fire screen flat on the floor or a table. Carefully cut out a large selection of reproduction 19th-century images and motifs from the paper frames that hold them in place, using a pair of short, straight-bladed scissors. Starting with the perimeter of the screen, loose-lay the border motifs in position, making additional cuts where necessary to ensure an even fit. Then repeat for the middle of the screen, working from top to bottom.

Choosing where to place the images, the degree to which you overlap them, and when and where to make additional cuts is largely a matter of personal composition. However, the most effective results are invariably produced by choosing darker coloured images for the border, gradually moving from lighter to darker ones as you work your way from the top to the bottom of the middle of the screen, and by ensuring that only very small sections of the green basecoat remain uncovered.

4 Once you are satisfied with the composition, carefully remove the cut outs and temporarily reposition them on a table-top or a large sheet of paper on the floor. Then, using an adhe-

7

sive such as cow gum or spray mount, fix them permanently to the screen in the same sequence as in 3 above. Apply adhesive right up to the edges of each cut out, or they may curl up away from the screen later on.

5 Once the adhesive has dried thoroughly, apply one or two coats of varnish for protection. To "antique" the surface, as here,

use a mid-dark-brown coloured French polish (or shellac).

6 The varnished screen should be left to dry thoroughly – impressions left by fingers and thumbs in tacky varnish can be impossible to remove.

7 Finally, insert the screen into the slots in the feet and position on the tiles at the front of the hearth.

Dressing a fireplace

Once you have installed or restored a period fire-place you will want to adorn it with appropriate fireplace impedimenta and decorative items. Here and on the following pages are some examples of period fireplaces that have been dressed in an authentic period fashion.

To dress a fireplace in a period style you first need to assemble the various implements necessary for the preparation and maintainance of the fire itself. They include andirons, fire-baskets, firebacks, fenders, shovels, brushes, tongs, bellows and coal scuttles. (See pages 18-77 for

Left: An elegant early Georgian wooden chimney-piece. The hearth is adorned with an ornate pair of andirons, a decorative cast-iron fireback and a pierced steel fender. On the fairly shallow mantel shelf ceramic blue and white pots are flanked by a pair of blue and white vases (these could be used as spill-holders). In addition to a large medallion-shaped portrait surmounted by a gilded eagle, the wood-panelled chimney breast is defined by an extensive and intricate nut garland, hung in the typical Classical manner of a swag-and-tails.

Right: In this authentic recreation of a Victorian parlour, the mantel shelf of the chimneypiece has been dressed with a chimney cloth. They were first used on Dutch fireplaces during the 17th century, and originally intended to reduce the amount of smoke entering the room. For the Victorians, however, they were, first and foremost, yet another decorative embellishment of the fireplace.

reference as to which ones are appropriate to particular periods.)

Traditionally, aside from these impedimenta, the hearth was kept relatively free from additional ornamentation because of the dirt, dust and smoke from the fire. The only notable exception to this was during the "High Victorian" period, when all manner of decorative objects and collectables were displayed. Outside of this era, accessories tended to be limited to wrought-iron jugs or bottle warmers, pairs of vases and decorative fire screens. During the summer months it was usual to install a fire screen, an arrangement of flowers or a paper fan.

Georgian fireplaces invariably had fairly shallow mantel shelves; consequently, displays should be restricted. For instance, you could have a clock flanked by a pair of candlesticks, while a mirror, a picture or a print, could be hung on the chimney breast. Mirrors are

Left: *A late-Victorian marble fireplace. Apart from the carved brackets supporting the mantel shelf, the surround is, from a decorative point of view, quite understated. The gleaming brass fire accessories in the hearth, however, are quite the opposite, and not untypical for the period. The combination of a gilt wooden overmantel mirror, central clock and flanking candleholders and vases also make a typically bold and ostentateous "High Victorian" statement.*

Right: *A fine example of an Arts and Crafts beaten copper fireplace, c.1904, by George Walton. Typical embellishments include a painting on the overmantel in its 1901 beaten copper frame, and an Arts and Crafts bowl, boxes and candlesticks – the latter by Christopher Dresser. The grate is by Charles Voysey.*

Right: *This simple wooden and brick fireplace is decorated with a selection of coloured glass dating from the 18th and 19th centuries, and an amusing collection of "mantel" dogs. The chimney breast above is covered with an extensive collection of prints, framed simply in black. Displaying collections on the mantel shelf (and even in the hearth) was a typical element of the "High Victorian" interior, and remains one of the essential ingredients when recreating a Victorian style in a room of today.*

particularly appropriate both as decoration and to reflect light back into the room.

On the wider and deeper mantel shelves of Regency and Victorian fireplaces you could display mantel clocks (under a glass dome), candlesticks adorned with lustres, spill-holders and pairs of vases. If you want too create a typical "High Victorian" look, the array of assembled objects can dramatically increase to include bowls, plates, ceramic figures, fans, dried flowers, busts, cameos, fossils, early photographs and all manner of knick-knacks. As

previously mentioned, displays can also spill over into the hearth and also onto overmantels that incorporate shelving.

The reaction to the "clutter" of the Victorian mantel shelf began among followers of the Aesthetic and Arts and Crafts Movement during the last quarter of the 19th century, and was echoed in the Modernist interiors of the 20th century. This resulted in a return to more minimal displays of earlier periods, with the emphasis, for the most part, on quality rather than quantity.

Glossary

Acanthus: A carved ornament of conventionalized, serrated leaves, used on Corinthian and Composite columns and mouldings.

Adamesque: A fireplace in the neo-Classical style, first introduced in Britain by the Adam brothers during the second half of the 18th century.

Aesthetic Movement: A decorative arts movement with a strong Japanese influence, which flourished in Britain from *c.*1870 to the late 1880s. A precursor of Art Nouveau, it also overlapped with the Arts and Crafts Movement.

Andirons: *See* Firedogs.

Anthemion: A classical ornament showing a repeating pattern of honeysuckle flowers and foliage.

Anthracite: A hard coal, consisting almost entirely of carbon, that burns nearly without a flame or smoke.

Architrave: A moulded framework; in Classical architecture, the lowest part of an entablature.

Art Deco: A style of decorative art particularly associated with the

1920s and 1930s, which developed the curvilinearity of Art Nouveau into more streamlined geometrical forms.

Art Nouveau: A style of decoration characterized by curves and flowing lines, asymmetry and flower and leaf motifs, prevalent from the 1880s to 1914.

Art Pauvre: *See* découpage.

Arts and Crafts Movement: Led by a group of artists and craftsmen, from approximately 1860 to 1925, who rejected machine-made, mass-produced items in favour of those made by traditional methods. Drew on pre-industrial periods and styles for inspiraton. One of the founder members was William Morris.

Bacchic: Decorative figures, jovial or drunken, and relating to Bacchus, the Greek and Roman god of wine.

Baronial style: Also known as "monastic style". Popular during the late 19th century and refers to a heavy, mock-Gothic style of architecture, decoration and furniture that drew on ecclesiastical designs, particularly Medieval.

Baroque: An extravagant and heavily ornate style of architecture, furniture and decoration that originated in 17th-century Italy.
Characterized by an abundant use of cupids, cornucopia and similar decorative motifs set in symmetrical, curvaceous designs. A precursor of the lighter and more frivolous and colourful Rococo style.

Bath stove: *See* Hob grate.

Beaux Arts Movement: Flourished in the United States between 1876 and 1930, and encompassed a variety of historical architectural styles. Led by American architects, such as Richard Morris Hunt, who had studied at the Ecole des Beaux Arts in Paris. Styles included French and Italian Renaissance (notably François Premier style), and Elizabethan, Georgian, Regency, English Gothic and Spanish revival, all allied with modern technology and methods of construction.

Billet: A small log of wood, a metal bar, and an ornament in Norman architecture in the form of short cylinders or blocks that have spaces between them.

Black-leading: A black coloured mineral (plumbago) used to polish cast-iron grates and ranges.

Bolection mouldings: A moulding covering the uneven joints made by two members of sections of different sizes, popular during the late 17th and 18th centuries.

Broken pediment: A pediment with a gap in the crown, sometimes filled with a motif such as an urn.

Cameo: A decoration with a figure (usually a bust or head in profile) carved in relief, and sometimes against a contrasting coloured background.

Capital: The head or top part of a column or pilaster.

Cartouche: A panel or tablet in round or oval form, often used for an inscription or coat of arms.

Caryatid: A human figure, usually female, supporting an entablature. (Male figures were referred to as atlantes.)

Chamfer: The surface created by cutting off the corner of a square, usually at a 45° angle.

Cheeks: The sloping sides of a fireplace opening.

Chevron: A V-shaped heraldic symbol representing two rafters of a house butting up to each other at an angle.

Chimney board: A device, usually made of wood, and elaborately decorated in paint, for blocking off the fireplace opening during the summer months (when the fire was unlit) to stop draughts entering the room from the flue.

Chimney breast: The stone, brick or cement structure that projects into a room and contains the fireplace flue.

Chimneypiece: A fireplace surround and its overmantel.

Chinoiserie: A European interpretation of Chinese art, popular from the late 17th to the 19th century.

Chippendale style: Furniture and architectural fixtures and fittings made to the designs of Thomas Chippendale (1718-89). His work showed a variety of influences, including Chinese, Rococo and Gothic styles.

Classicism: A revival or a return to the principles of Greek or Roman art and architecture. Can be seen in the Carolingian renovation of the late Imperial Roman architecture, during the 8th and 9th centuries; also the Tuscan Proto-Renaissance of the 11th century; the 16th-century Renaissance; the 17th century Baroque and later Rococo; the work of Perrault and Mansart in late 17th-century France, and of Colen Campbell, Lord Burlington and William Kent in early 18th-century England, who led a return to Classicism via the earlier work of Inigo Jones and Palladio; this Palladianism has been considered as the first phase of the late 18th-century neo-Classical movement.

Neo-Classicism began in the 1750s as a reaction to the excesses of the late Baroque and Rococo, and can best be seen in Piranesi's etchings depicting a new vision of Roman architecture emphasising its formal and spatial motifs, and rejecting earlier "incorrect" Classical motifs. This led to an appreciation of the more austere Greek Doric and, in turn, to Greek revivalism. Neo-Classical architecture is solid rather than severe, and decoration is restrained or eliminated altogether.

In the early 19th century such Classical ideas were abandoned in favour of styles richer in decoration and more picturesque in composition, as exemplified in the luxurious and dramatic Roman Imperial style of French architecture under the Empire. Throughout the rest of the 19th century, revivals of Greek, Roman and Renaissance Classicism went in and out of fashion at various points in time.

Colonial style: An all-embracing term used to describe architecture, fixtures and fittings and furniture made in a style prevalent in the North American Colonies from the early 17th-century pioneer settlements to the establishment of a Federal Government in 1789.

Column: A vertical member, circular in section and normally with a gentle taper (entasis). In Classical architecture it is composed of a base, shaft and capital.

Composition: A mixture of paper or wood pulp, whiting and glue, moulded into decorative motifs and applied to the surface of fire-surround or overmantel.

Console: A decorative scroll-shaped bracket.

Corbel: A projecting stone or timber block, often carved, supporting a horizontal member such as mantel shelf or beam.

Corinthian: An ornate style of Greek architecture, originally from Corinth; notable features include acanthus capitals on columns.

Cornice: In Classical architecture, the projecting top of an entablature.

Curb: The fixed framework that encloses a raised fireplace hearth.

Cusps: The projecting points formed where foils meet in Gothic tracery.

Deal: A softwood, invariably fir or pine.

Découpage: The craft of applying decorative paper cut-outs to a wide range of surfaces which originated in the 18th century.

Delftware: A form of earthenware, such as glazed tiles for fireplace slips, originally made in Delft, Holland.

Dentil: One of a series of small blocks used to form an ornamental row, and primarily used in Corinthian, Ionic and Composite mouldings. The collective term is dentillations, or a dentillated cornice.

Diaperwork: An overall pattern of small, repeated motifs, usually of diagonal, lozenge form.

Dog grate: A free-standing basket grate.

Early Georgian: A style of architecture and decoration prevalent in England between 1714 and 1740.

Ebonized: Wood stained and polished black to simulate ebony.

Edwardian: A style of architecture and decoration prevalent in England between 1901 and 1910.

Egg-and-dart moulding: A decorative moulding carved with a series of alternating rounded ovals and arrowheads.

Elizabethan style: A style of architecture and decoration prevalent in England during the 17th century.

Empire style: A style popular in France between 1804–30, and in the United States between 1810–30. It is characterized by the use of sombre, heavy-looking woods, such as mahogany, ebony and rosewood which were mostly uncarved but generously ornamented with motifs such as burning torches, urns, lions' masks, eagles and swans, papyrus leaves, crocodiles, sphinxes and other Egyptian motifs. In the United States the style was adapted to include local motifs such as fruit, flowers and the American eagle.

Enamelling: A technique for applying (and firing) a vitrified, glossy coating to metal, wooden and ceramic surfaces.

Encaustic tiles: Earthenware tiles patterned with inlays of coloured clay slips.

Engaged columns: A column or half-column attached to a surface behind, such as a jamb or wall.

Entablature: In Classical architecture the top of an Order, made up of an architrave, frieze and cornice.

Etruscan style: A late 18th-century offshoot of neo-Classicism introduced by Robert Adam *c.*1774, and based on the architecture, ornamental wares and style of decoration originating in Etruria (now Tuscany and Umbria), an ancient Italian state north of the River Tiber.

Faïence: Tin-glazed earthenware.

Fascia: A horizontal band in an entablature.

Faux marble: The art of simulating marble using paints and glazes.

Federal style: Architecture, fixtures and fittings, furniture and a style of decoration from the early years of American independence

(1789–1830); often incorporates patriotic and military symbols, such as the eagle.

Fender: A screen or guard placed in front of a fireplace to prevent hot coals from falling onto the surrounding floor or carpet.

Festoon: *See* Swag.

Finial: An ornament on top of an upright or vertical section of, for example, an andiron or register grate.

Firedogs: Supports for logs in a fireplace; also called andirons.

Fire irons: Fireplace tools, such as a shovel, poker and tongs.

Fireback: A thick iron plate placed at the back of a hearth to protect the wall and reflect heat into the room.

Flue: A cavity in a chimney breast, or a pipe, used to convey smoke, hot gases and flames from a fire to outside of a building.

Fluting: Shallow vertical grooves on the shaft of a column.

Foil: A lobe or leaf-shaped curve formed between cusps inside an arch or circle.

Foliated: Decorated with carved leaves.

François Premier style: A style of architecture and decoration popular in the United States during the Beaux Arts period, and modelled on French Renaissance châteaux; notable features included enormous, hooded stone fireplaces.

French Empire style: *See* Empire style *and* Classicism.

Frieze: The middle section of an entablature, or the panel below the mantel shelf, between the jambs and above the fireplace opening.

Fumed oak: Oak darkened by ammonia fumes.

Gable: The part of the wall immediately under the end of a pitched roof, cut into a triangular shape by the sloping sides of the roof.

Georgian style: An 18th-century style that is characterized by the use of proportions and ornaments of Classical architecture.

Gesso: A plaster of Paris used either to create a smooth surface, usually on wood, prior to painted, or to mould applied decorative motifs.

Gilding: A wafer-thin covering of gold leaf, or a gold-like substance.

Gothic: A style of architecture and design which

flourished from the 11th to the 15th century, and was characterized by soaring, slender lines, pointed or ogee arches and tracery.

Gothick: 18th and early 19th century spelling of Gothic, denoting today the delicate applied ornament which was fashionable before the full-scale Gothic revival of 1840 onward.

Gothic revival: A 19th-century revival, led by Augustus Pugin, William Burges, William Morris, and Charles Eastlake, of Gothic forms and motifs.

Gougework: An ornamental pattern made in wood with a rounded chisel.

Greek key pattern: A geometrical decoration made of continuous right-angled lines. It is also known as Greek meander.

Greek revival: A fashion for Greek architecture, and its simplicity and gravity, began in the 1780s, and culminated in a Greek Revival in Britain, Europe and America in the 1820s and '30s; best seen in the work of Ledoux and Soane.

Guilloche: Decoration of interlaced bands, forming a pattern of circles or loops.

Hearth: The floor of a fireplace, usually extending out into a room.

Herm: A head of bust on a rectangular pillar.

High Victorian: Commonly refers to a style of decoration in which furniture, soft furnishings, decorative objects, and decoration in general were richly ornamented, coloured and patterned. Most interiors were packed with all manner of furnishings and objects – a style popular during the third quarter of the 19th century, and one that came to be rejected as "clutter" by members of the Aesthetic and Arts and Crafts Movement.

Hob: A ledge on the back or side of a fireplace or grate used for warming a pot or kettle.

Hob grate: A cast-iron grate in which the fire basket is supported off the ground, between two flat hobs. The flat front is usually cast with shallow ornament or reeding. Known as a Bath stove in the United States.

Incised: Deeply engraved or carved.

Inglenook: A recessed space beside a fireplace, usually housing one or two benches.

Ionic: One of the Classical orders of archi-tecture, characterized by fluted columns and prominent volutes on the capitals.

Jacks: A mechanical device for rotating meat on a spit.

Jacobean: Style of architecture, fixtures and fittings and decoration characteristic of the period of James I of England (1603-25).

Jacobethan: Style of architecture, furniture and decoration characteristic of the reigns of Elizabeth I and James I of England.

Jambs: The vertical sides of a fireplace, usually supporting the horizontal mantel shelf.

Late Georgian: Style of architecture and decoration prevalent in England between 1760 and 1790.

Latticework: A network of crossed laths or bars.

Linefold panelling: Wooden panelling in which the individual panels are carved with a motif that looks like the vertical folds of linen; originates from the Tudor period.

Lintel: A supporting wood or stone beam across the top of the fireplace opening.

Louis Quatorze-style: A style inspired by the Court of the Sun King, Louis XIV (1643–1715) and his palace at Versailles. Broadly, it consisted of a more opulent Baroque modified by Classical lines and marked by flamboyant craftsmanship and the use of exotic woods and inlays.

Louis Quinze-style: (1720-50) – *See* Rococo style.

Louis Seize-style: A (Greek) Classical reaction to the fussiness of Rococo that began 20 years before Louis XVI-style, in 1754.

Lustres: A candlestick of vase ornamented with pendants of cut-glass.

Lyre: A harp-like musical instrument, notably used in ancient Greece as an accompaniment to poetry.

Majolica: A form of earthenware painted to look like the colourful glazes of 16th-century Italian majolica.

Mantel shelf: The horizontal shelf above the fireplace opening.

MDF: Medium density fibreboard, made from compressed particles of wood and used in the construction of furniture and various architectural fixtures and fittings.

Medallion: *See* Rose.

Medieval: Commonly used to refer to that period of European history known as the Middle Ages (476 AD, the fall of the last Western Roman emperor, Constantine, to 1453, the start of the Italian Renaissance.

Mid-Georgian: Style of architecture and decoration prevalent in England from 1740 to 1760.

Milk paint: Also known as buttermilk or cassein paint. Made by mixing earth-coloured pigments with buttermilk or skimmed milk, and a little lime (the latter for its insecticidal or fungicidal properties). Particularly popular in country areas of North America during the late 18th and 19th century, and commonly found in Colonial-style interiors.

Modernism: A self-conscious style created by architects of the Modern Movement, inspired by a need to break with the past and to express the spirit of a new machine age. Rejected ornamentation in favour of space, proporation and smooth surfaces. Began c.1920 and had been generally rejected by c.1960.

Mosaic: A design or pattern made up of different coloured pieces of material, usually marble but also glass.

Neo-Classical style: A style of architecture, fixtures and fittings and decoration based on the forms of ancient Greece and Rome. Characteristic elements include chains of Classical motifs such as garlands of flowers, palmettes, anthemions, round and oval paterae, urns and cameos. Also see Classicism.

Nursery cock: A gas tap with a removable on/off key.

Overmantel: A decorative treatment above a fireplace, often incorporating a painting or mirror.

Palladian style: An interpretation of the Classical style developed by the Italian architect Andrea Palladio (1508–80). Palladianism was bought to England by Inigo Jones in the 17th century, revived in the early 18th century by Lord Burlington and Colen Campbell, and influenced American architecture in the late 18th century.

Palmette: A decorative motif based on the fan-shaped leaf of a palm tree.

Pargeting: Plasterwork.

Paterae: Small oval or round ornaments in Classical architecture, often decorated with flowers or leaves.

Pattern book: A book containing drawings and designs for architecture, furniture, fixtures and fittings, and styles of decoration.

Pediment: A triangular-shaped decorative section over a fireplace; if it has an open top it is called a broken pediment.

Pier: The support for a lintel or an arch.

Pilaster: A flat rectangular Classical column.

Pompeian: In the style of architecture and artefacts discovered during excavations at Pompeii in Italy, which began in 1748.

Porphyry: A hard, fine-grained rock flecked with white crystals; predominently either dark red, purple, grey or green in colour.

Post-Modernism: A reaction against Modernism. It began in the 1950s and promoted the reintroduction of bright colours and decoration, and architectural components that weren't necessarily functional.

Pulvinated: A section with a convex profile, usually a frieze.

Purdonium: A coal scuttle or bucket.

Putti: Cherubs or young boys used as a subject in Italian Renaissance decoration.

PVA: A water-based adhesive.

Quatrefoil: A four-lobed circle or arch formed by cusping.

Queen Anne revival style: A style of architecture popular during the second half of the 19th century, devised by Richard Norman Shaw and Eden Nesfield and inspired by mid-17th-century Dutch houses of Dutch influence and the William and Mary style (rather than Gothic and Tudor).

Reeding: A form of decoration created by narrow convex mouldings in parallel strips and divided by grooves.

Reformation: A religious and political movement in 16th-century Europe that began as an attempt to reform the Roman Catholic Church and resulted in the establishment of the Protestant Churches.

Regency: Styles of architecture, furniture and decoration popular during 1811–20.

Register grate: A fire grate with a moveable iron plate in the flue to regulate the updraught.

Renaissance: The flowering of Classical

scholarship, scientific and geographical discovery, and the assertion of the active and secular over the religious and contemplative life, at the end of the Middle Ages.

Restoration: The re-establishment of the monarchy in 1660 in Britain; also the reign of Charles II (1660–85).

Rocaille: Shell and irregular stone decoration popular in the Rococo style.

Rococo: A style of architecture and decoration first popularized in France, in the 1720s. Rococo embraces shell, foliage, delicately curved forms of ornamentation unrelated to the underlying structure.

Rose: A moulded, circular-shaped, decorative feature, known in the United States as a medallion.

Rosette: Any rose-shaped ornament.

Roundel: A round flat ornament.

Rubbed brick: Carved brickwork.

Scagliola: A decorative finish imitating marble and made from hardened and polished plaster and marble chips.

Scroll: A partly coiled or curved decorative feature

in plaster, wood, marble, or virtually any other material; looks like a rolled up piece of parchment.

Sepiolite: A powder which is used to make up a poultice for cleaning marble, slate and other stones. Available from chemists.

Serpentine: A snakelike winding edge, for example, to the front of a mantel shelf.

Shingle-style: North American houses with exterior walls clad with wooden tiles.

Slips: A fascia set into a fire-surround (usually marble or tiles).

Spandrels: The approximately triangular-shaped space between the curve of an arch and the rectangular frame above it.

Spill-holder: A container for small strips or tapers of wood and paper used to light fires, candles and pipes.

Stop-chamfer: A triangular termination to a chamfer, bringing a three-sided form back to a right angle.

Strapwork: Decoration formed by interlaced strips, either applied or carved in wood, stone or plaster, and associated with Gothic architecture.

Stucco: A fine cement of plaster used for decorative motifs.

Swag: A carved or painted decoration resembling a piece of fabric draped between two supports; or a garland of ribbons, flowers, fruit and/or foliage. (Also known as a festoon.)

Tablets: A panel, usually intended for a decorative inscription.

Tour de cheminees: A chimney cloth, hung from the mantel shelf and designed to minimize the amount of smoke entering the room from the hearth; also a decorative item.

Tracery: An ornamental arrangement of intersecting ribwork, forming a pierced pattern.

Transparent oil glaze: A viscous, clear medium to which pigments are added to form a semi-transparent glaze or paint.

Trefoil: A three-lobed circle or arch formed by cusping.

Trimmer: A small horizontal beam below a floor into which the ends of joists are framed.

Trivet: A bracket with three projections for fixing on the top bar of a grate, and used to support a pot or kettle.

Tudor: Styles of architecture and decoration prevalent during the reigns of the Tudor monarchs (1485-1601).

Volutes: Scroll-shaped brackets.

Wattle-and-daub: Wattlework (interwoven branches or pieces of wood) plastered with mud and used as a building material, usually for making walls.

William IV: Style of architecture, furniture and decoration during the reign of William IV (1830–37).

Woodgraining: The art of simulating the appearance of natural wood, and particularly the grain and figuring, using paints and glazes.

Directory

ARCHITECTURAL SALVAGE

Architectural Antiques
351 Kings Road
London W6 9NH
Antique and reproduction marble fire-surrounds, plus installation and restoration of antique and new marble.

Architectural Heritage
Taddington Manor
Taddington
Nr Cutsdean
Cheltenham
Gloucestershire GL54 5RY
Suppliers of a large and varied collection of period chimneypieces.

Au Temps Perdu
5 Stapleton Road
Bristol BS5 0QR
Architectural salvage, antiques and building materials, mostly from France. Many items restored. Shipping and installation can be arranged.

Baileys Architectural Antiques
The Engine Shed
Ashburton Industrial Estate
Ross on Wye
Herefordshire HR9 7BW
A large and changing inventory of decorative architectural items for the house, authentic and reproduction, including fireplaces, mantelpieces and tiles.

Cantabrian Antiques
16 Park Street
Lynton
North Devon
Reclaimed architectural items, including fire-places and tiles.

Conservation Building Products
Forge Works
Forge Lane
Cradley Heath
Warley
West Midlands B64 5AL
Salvaged and new build-ing materials for period buildings, including fire-places and accessories.

Crowther of Syon Lodge
Syon Lodge
Busch Corner
London Road
Isleworth
Middlesex TW7 5BH
Restored antiques from around the world, including fireplaces.

The London Architectural Salvage and Supply Co Ltd
St Michael's
Mark Street
London EC2 4ER
A large selection of fire-places in wood, stone and marble.

Michael Main Ltd
The Old Rectory
Cerrig-y-Drudion
Corwen
North Wales
LL21 0RU
Architectural antiques, including fireplaces.

Tatters of Tyseley Ltd
590 Warwick Road
Tyseley
Birmingham B11 2HJ
Architectural antiques of all kinds, with nation-wide delivery; restoration services include complete fireplace fitting and dec-orative paint finishes and marbling to surrounds and interiors.

Walcot Reclamation
108 Walcot Street
Bath
A large selection of archi-tectural antiques and building materials from all periods, including tiles, chimneypots and fireplaces. Restoration work also done.

SPECIALIST FIRE-PLACE COMPANIES

Acquisitions
269 Camden High Street
London NW1 7BX
Original and reproduc-tion Victorian and Edwardian fireplaces and accessories.

Amazing Grates
61–3 High Road
East Finchley
London N2 8AB
Manufacturers of repro-duction fireplace settings and suppliers of original chimneypieces and insert grates. Stock includes wood and marble man-tels, fireplace tiles and a wide range of accessories.

The Amazing Grate Company
Unit 7
Avon Gorge Centre
Portview Road
Avonmouth
Bristol
Avon BS11 9LQ
Authentic reproductions of original fireplaces, using traditional materi-als. Also solid brass fend-ers and reproduction Victorian tiles.

Ashburton Fireplaces
West Street
Ashburton
Devon TQ13 7DU
Authentic antique chim-neypieces in marble, wood and cast iron c.1790-1920. Fitting service available. Also makers of reproduction Georgian, Victorian and Edwardian cast-iron fire place inserts and acces-sories, marble and wood surrounds, hand-painted fireplace tiles in Victorian Arts and Crafts and Art Nouveau styles.

Britain's Heritage
Shaftesbury Hall
3 Holy Bones
Leicester
Large selection of restored original fireplaces.

The Ceramic Stove Company
4 Earl Street
Oxford OX2 0JA
Specializes in tile-clad wood-burning stoves from Scandinavia.

Chapel House Fireplaces
Netherfield House
St George's Road
Scholes Holmfirth
West Yorkshire
Original Victorian fire-places. More than 400 cast-iron models in stock, and mantel shelves in oak, pine and mahogany, iron and marble. Viewing by appointment only.

Dowding Metalcraft Ltd
Mulberry Road
Canvey Island
Essex SS8 0PR
Manufactureres of repro-duction fire grates and fenders for wood, coal, gas and electric fires.

Firestyle Chimneypieces
158 Upminster Road
Upminster
Essex RM14 2RB
Handcrafted marble chimneypieces in several Classical and period designs; also fireplace inserts and a fitting service available.

Grahamston Iron Company
PO Box 5
Gowan Avenue
Falkirk
Stirlingshire FK2 7HH
Ironfounders and enam-ellers of fireplace inserts, grates and stoves.

Hallidays
The Old College
Dorchester-on-Thames
Oxfordshire OX9 8HL
Specialize in hand-

crafted Baltic pine reproduction mantel-piece designs of the Regency, Georgian, Victorian and Edwardian periods. Also, marble slips, hearths, grates, fenders and other acces-sories, both reproduction and original.

Hilton Forge Ltd
Hilton Village
Derbyshire DE6 5SE
Quality reproduction Victorian cast-iron fire-places. Their "Victorian Classic Fireplace" collec-tion features designs taken from 1827–1901.

Ideal Fireplaces
62 South Parade
Chiswick
London W4
Suppliers of reproduction and authentic English and French marble fire-places, cast-iron and tiled Victorian inserts and Georgian and Victorian style mantel-pieces made from new and reclaimed pine. Overmantel mirrors, fire screens and other repro-duction accessories also available.

Morley Marketing
PO Box 38
Ware
Hertfordshire
SG12 7JP
Stockists of wood- and coal-burning stoves.

Mr Wandle's Workshop
200-202 Garratt Lane
London SW18 4ED
Suppliers and restorers

of authentic Victorian cast-iron fireplaces, grates and accessories. Also Victorian kitchen ranges and stoves.

Nostalgia
61 Shaw Heath
Stockport
Cheshire SK3 8BH
Fully restored Victorian fireplaces and fireplace accessories.

Old Flames
30 Long Street
Easingwood
York
Fully restored Victorian fireplaces.

Original Features
155 Tottenham Lane
Crouch end
London N8 9BT
Reproduction fireplaces and accessories; plus an installation service.

Overmantels
66 Battersea Bridge Road
London SW11 3AG
Overmantel mirrors reproduced from Victorian, Regency and French originals.

Petit Rouge
5a New Road
Croxley Green
Rickmansworth
Hertfordshire
WD3 3EJ
Makers of Georgian and Regency style mantel-pieces in hand-carved pine and polished sheet marble. Coloured mar-bles and granites can be specially ordered. Also, cast-iron, wrought iron

and brass grates and other accessories for wood- and coal-burning fireplaces.

Replicas
262-268 South Road
Walkley
Sheffield
Suppliers of cast-iron inserts of tiled, arched or keyhole types. Also fire-surrounds, fenders and accessories.

Stovay Ltd
Falcon Road
Sowten Industrial Estate
Exeter
Devon EX2 7LF
Suppliers of reproduction cast-iron 19th-century fireplaces with authentic recreations of Victorian hearth tiles, surrounds and fenders. Also supply cast-iron stoves.

T F Buckle
427 Kings Road
Chelsea
London SW10 0LR
Reproduction and antique period mantel-pieces in a wide range of styles and sizes in hand-carved solid pine and marble. Plus a selection of decorative tile inserts.

The Victorian Fireplace
Thanet House
92 Broad Street
Canterbury
Kent
Over 150 period fire-places in stock; also supply gas fires and pro-vide an installation and restoration service.

UK Marble Ltd
21 Burcott ROad
Hereford
HR4 9LW
*Marble and granite for
fireplaces and other
architectural fixtures
and fittings.*

Winther Browne
Nobel Road
Eley Estate
London
N18 3DX
*Specialize in decorative
wooden carvings and
mouldings for mantel-
pieces in pine and
mahogany, but other
timbers can be ordered.
Items not illustrated in
their catalogue can also
be commissioned.*

**Wye Valley Stoves and
Fireplaces**
Palma Court
Brookend Street
Ross on Wye
Herefordshire
HR9 7EE
*Cast-iron stoves and
fireplaces, including
Victorian originals. Plus
firebacks, fenders, coal
scuttles, tiles and other
accessories.*

**REPRODUCTION AND
ORIGINAL TILES**

**The British Ceramic
Tile Council**
Federation House
Station Road
Stoke-on-Trent
Staffordshire
ST4 2RT
*Offer advice on all
aspects of tiles and
tiling.*

**Campbell Ceramic
Fireplace Tiles**
H & R Johnson Tiles Ltd
Highgate Tile Works
Tunstall
Stoke-on-Trent
Staffordshire
ST6 4JX
*Victorian reproduction
fire tile panels, decora-
tive borders and insets
and co-ordinating
hearth tiles*

Castelnau Tiles
175 Church Road
Barnes
London SW13 9R
*Stockists of reproduction
period tiles.*

Decorative Tile Works
Jackfield Tile Museum
Ironbridge
Telford
Shropshiire TF8 7AW
*Specialists in the repro-
duction of 19th-century
English tiles*

Dennis Ruabon Ltd
Haford Tileries
Ruabon
Wrexham
Clwyd LL14 6ET
*Manufacturers of a wide
selection of tiles, including many traditional
"paver" shapes, such as
"bats", "sinters" and
"quoirns", which can be
laid to create an exten-
sive range of geometric
tiling patterns*

Fired Earth
Twyford Mill
Oxford Road
Adderbury
Oxfordshire OX17 3HP
*Terracotta , slate and
limestone floor tiles, and*

*traditional wall and fire-
place tiles.*

Interior Ceramics
3 York Street
Twickenham
Middlesex TQ1 3JZ
*Comprehensive selection
of ceramic tiles, marble,
terracotta and slate;
Victorian reproduction
and hand-painted tiles
are a speciality*

John Burgess Tiles
Unit B25
Maws Craft Centre
Jackfield
Shropshire TF8 7LS
*Reproduction Victorian
and Art Nouveau tiles.*

**Kenneth Clark
Ceramics**
The North Wing
Southover Grange
Southover Road
Lewes
East Sussex BN17 1TP
*Manufacturers and
stockists of an extensive
range of reproduction
tiles; also stock some
original tiles*

**Marston and
Langinger**
192 Ebury Street
London SW1N 8UP
*Wide selection of period
tiles*

**The Original Tile
Company**
23a Howe Street
Edinburgh EH3 6TF
*Wide range of wall and
floor tiles, including terracotta, natural stone,
marble and hand-paint-
ed, in many period
styles.*

Bibliography

Addy, Sidney Oldall, *The Evolution of the English House*, The Macmillan Company (1898)

Airs, Malcolm, *The Buildings of Britian: Tudor and Jacobean*, Barrie and Jenkins (1982)

Barrett, Helena, and Phillips, John, *Suburban Style*, Macdonald Orbis (1987)

Beeton, Mrs. *Book of Household Management*, London (1906)

Calder, Jenni, *The Victorian Home*, Batsford (1977)

Calloway, Stephen, *The Elements of Style*, Mitchell Beazley (1991)

Calloway, Stephen, and Jones, Stephen, *Traditional Style* Pyramid Books (1990)

Clark, Robert Judson, *The Arts and Crafts Movement in America 1876-1916* Princeton University Press (1973)

Cook, Olive, *The English House through Seven Centuries*, Penguin Books (1984)

Griffith, Helen C., *Southern Interiors*, Oxmoor House (1988)

Hamlin, Talbot, *Greek Revival Architecture in America*, Oxford University Press (1944)

Hartley, Dorothy, *Food in England*, Futura (1985)

Hills, Nicholas, *The English Fireplace*, Quiller Press (1983)

Johnson, Alan, *How to Restore and Improve Your Victorian House*, David & Charles (1984)

Kyle Leopold, Allison, *Victorian Splendour*, Stewart, Tabori & Chang, New York (1986)

Lloyd, Nathanial, *A History of the English House*, The Architectural Press (1975)

McDonald, Roxana, *The Fireplace Book*, The Architectural Press (1984)

Miller, Martin and Judith,
– *Period Details*, Mitchell Beazley (1987)
– *Period Finishes and Effects*, Mitchell Beazley (1992)
– *Period Style*, Mitchell Beazley (1989)
– *Victorian Style*, Mitchell Beazley (1993)

Muthesius, Hermann, *Das Englische Hous*, Berlin (1904)

Shuffrey, L.A., *The English Fireplace*, Batsford (1912)

Thornton, Peter, *Authentic Decor: The Domestic Interior 1620–1920*, George Weidenfeld and Nicholson Ltd (1984)

West, Trudy, *The Fireplace in the Home*, David and Charles (1976)

Wood, Margaret, *The English Medieval House*, Ferndale Editions (1981)

Index

ACKNOWLEDGEMENTS

The author and publishers would like to thank the following organisations and individuals for providing the photographs used in this book:

Crowther of Syon Lodge, MJM Publishing Projects, Caroline Brown, Geoff Dann, John Helfrick, Martin Miller, *Period Living* and *Traditional Homes*, Stewart Grant, Reed International Books Ltd, Paul Bricknell, Michael Crockett, Dennis and Sheila Curran, Ian B. Jones, James Merrell, Kim Sayer.

Thanks to Mamelok Press Ltd, Northern Way, Bury St Edmunds, Suffolk IP32 6NJ for providing the paper scraps for the Victorian fire screen and thanks also to the following antique dealers who kindly supplied us with props for photography:

Constance Stobo
31 Holland Street
London W8 4NA

Clare Hobson
P.O. Box 960
London SW6 5XA

Hart & Rosenberg
2–3 Gateway Arcade
Camden Passage
London N1 0PD

Buckingham Antique Fireplaces
194/200 Battersea Park Road
London SW11

Rosemary Hart
4 Gateway Arcade
Camden Passage
London N1 0PG

The Dining Room Shop
62-4 White Hart Lane
London SW13 0PZ

Heartfelt thanks to Roderick Meborn-Hubbard for all his hard work.